Sleeve Puppets

Sleeve Puppets

Brenda Morton

with drawings by Juliet Renny

FABER AND FABER
London   Boston

*First published in 1978
by Faber and Faber Limited
3 Queen Square London WC1
Printed in Great Britain by
BAS Printers Limited
Over Wallop, Hampshire
All rights reserved*

British Library Cataloguing in Publication Data

Morton, Brenda
  Sleeve puppets.
  1. Puppet making
  I. Title
  745.59'22   TT174.7

  ISBN 0-571-11145-9
  ISBN 0-571-11250-1   Pbk

Contents

Introduction

There are fashions in puppets. Current favourites are sleeve puppets with mouths that open to speak. These puppets are held openly on the puppeteer's arm. He can stand and hold them or sit with them on his knee. They have enormous scope as they can be used as ventriloquist's dummies with their own distinctive voices or can be silent, either miming to records or demonstrating their views by the way the mouth and head are manipulated. They can concentrate on sparkling dialogue or can indulge in wild antics and clowning without speaking. The present trend is towards puppets that have strong characters, ranging from mischievousness to hilarious wickedness.

To the needlewoman these puppets present a new field to explore. All are made by basic sewing techniques and provide a wide range of bird and animal characters. They are interesting to make but it is only when the sewing is finished that the real enchantment begins as the owner learns how to move the puppet to gain maximum effect, tries out different voices and has the thrill of watching the new personality develop.

Dressing the Puppets and *Design Your Own Puppets* sections (pages 114 to 117) show how to use the patterns to invent your own characters. So when you have made all the puppets in the book you have not finished—you have only just begun!

METRICATION

Dual measurements, imperial and metric, are given throughout the book. In most cases an exact conversion has been given. But in the *Materials* paragraph preceding the instructions for each individual puppet there are variations. $\frac{1}{4}$ yd equals about 22·85 cm but fabrics sold by the metre are cut to the nearest 10 cm. Thus $\frac{1}{4}$ yd is

9

converted to 30 cm. However, some of the parts can be made out of 20 cm and whenever possible this shorter length is quoted, so do not think a misprint has occurred if $\frac{1}{4}$ yd is converted as 30 cm in some places and 20 cm in others! The normal width of fabric remains roughly the same; the familiar 35/36 in width now being quoted as 90 cm.

No conversion is given for patterns shown on squared grids. Only use the measurement given as fractional differences in metric conversion could upset the pattern.

General Instructions

Working the Puppet's Mouth

Four fingers go into upper mouth or beak and thumb goes into lower mouth or beak.

Straight speaking When thumb and fingers are close together mouth is shut. As they open away from each other mouth opens to speak.

Other emotions If there are no padded parts above or below the basic mouth, the fingers can be screwed up and the thumb moved sideways to register disgust, disdain, a snarl and other emotions that add sparkle and amusement to the puppet's performance.

PATTERNS

PATTERNS SHOWN ON LINED SQUARES

Patterns which are on squares are too big to fit the page and must be squared up as follows.

Take a sheet of paper. Rule lines one inch apart across it and down it. To get accurate patterns it is better not to convert into cm in this case.

Copy the pattern shapes carefully onto the same number of squares on your ruled paper, crossing the lines at exactly the same places. You do not need to be an artist. Just follow the lines carefully from square to square.

PATTERNS WITH A PART MARKED 'FOLD'

Having traced the pattern or redrawn it onto one inch squares lay your pattern on folded paper and cut out. Unfold the paper and you have the full-size pattern. If two sides of pattern are marked 'Fold' fold a square of paper in half horizontally, then in half vertically.

Draw pattern. Cut out. When opened out full-size pattern results.

REVERSING PATTERN TO MAKE A PAIR

When cutting two pieces in fabric that has a right and a wrong side reverse the second piece in order to make a pair.

FABRICS

Any fabric that is not too loosely-woven or flimsy can be used for these puppets. If fabric is likely to fray, oversew edges of any part that is not being stuffed as soon as it is cut out, if you want your puppet to last.

Fur fabrics are very effective. Glass-headed pins are the safest to use on fur fabric as their round coloured heads make them less likely to be lost in the pile. Work on the back of the fabric when pinning patterns and cutting out. Arrows on patterns show direction in which pile should stroke. Tack seams with large oversewing stitches along the edges before sewing as furry sides just pinned together can slip badly. When puppet is made brush seams with a clean clothes brush to release the pile and give a professional finish or pick out the pile with a pin.

STITCHES

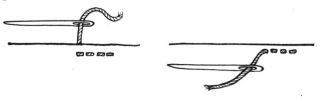

Stab-stitch Pull the thread taut at each stage to give smaller stronger stitches than running stitch.

14

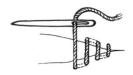

Ladder stitch Makes it easy to join limbs to body. To do ladder stitch take one small straight stitch on one part, then a small straight stitch on the other part. Keep the stitching moving in the same direction. Pull the thread tight every three or four stitches and the stitches will lace up and disappear, leaving a neat join that is very strong because there is no thread on the surface to be worn away. The drawing shows the stitches before the thread which laces it together is pulled tight.

Machining is an advantage for the larger puppets which have long seams. It is not specifically mentioned in the book but if you feel you can handle a machine round small tight curves it can be substituted for backstitch in most situations. The only place where machining is not recommended is when putting mouth or bill into body the first time you make a particular model. If the fit is wrong it is easier to undo hand sewing.

STUFFING

The modern polyester stuffings are excellent for puppets as they are light. Heavy stuffings should be avoided if possible. If the puppet sits on the puppeteer's knee weight is not too important, but if it is being held out the whole weight is carried by the hand at the end of an outstretched arm and that hand has to open and shut the mouth. After a few minutes there can be a feeling of strain if the stuffing is too heavy.

STUFFING STICK

Not essential, but a great help. Make one from a piece of dowel rod, rounded at one end and sharpened to a blunt point at the other. Or

15

use a thick knitting needle. Use it to guide stuffing into narrow parts. Also use it to help to turn out narrow limbs before stuffing.

EYES

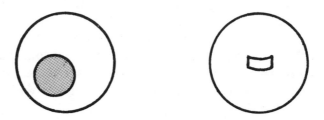

Joggle eyes made in white plastic with black centres that move are effective on these puppets. They are bought from handicraft shops and the 1 in (2·5 cm) size is recommended. The type used here has a shank on the back which is sewn to the fabric. These are not suitable for toddlers and babies who might bite them off but these puppets are not intended for these age-groups.

Home-made eyes Trace the circles given. Cut the large circle in white felt or interlining, the middle one in coloured felt and the small one in black felt. Using white thread sew middle of black circle to coloured circle. This gives highlights on pupil. Using coloured thread sew round edge of coloured circle onto white circle. Using white thread sew round edge of white circle onto puppet.

16

Standard Instructions

Sewing the Mouth or Beak

The actual shapes of mouths or beaks vary throughout the book but the basic method of making each one is the same. Instructions given here apply to each puppet.

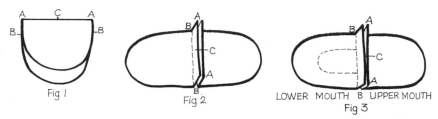

Fig 1

Fig 2

LOWER MOUTH B UPPER MOUTH
Fig 3

Fig. 1 Place upper and lower mouths on top of each other wrong sides to outside. Backstitch using thread double from A to B on each side. Mark point C on each mouth.

Fig. 2 Open out. The edges AB will stand up like a ridge. Place on top of inner mouth wrong sides to outside. Keeping ridge upright (this is the mouth opening that will be sewn into head) backstitch, using thread double, right round outside edge. Turn to right side through opening AA.

Fig. 3 Lay mouth flat, again with edges AB standing upright. Pin paper pattern for thumb pocket on lower mouth. Open end of thumb pocket lies at foot of ridge about $\frac{1}{2}$ in (1·2 cm) from line AA. Using thread to match the mouth sew small running stitches round the edge of the pattern, going through both thicknesses of lower and inner mouths. Leave straight edge open. Remove pattern. Put hand into mouth and check for fit as described next.

CHECKING FIT OF MOUTH OR BEAK

The areas provided for the fingers and thumb should fit comfortably but firmly. If they are too tight the puppet will be uncomfortable to operate. If they are too loose the puppeteer's fingers roll about uselessly and he does not have full control of the mouth. Check fit when mouth is made before it is sewn into head or body. Ideally make a mouth in old fabric and test it for fit before cutting into good fabric.

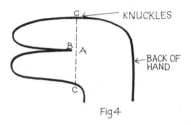

Fig 4

1. Test upper mouth for width. Adjust pattern if necessary. There will be more 'pull' on mouth when it is sewn into head so only adjust really bad looseness.
2. Test upper mouth for length. Fig. 4 shows open end of upper mouth just covering the knuckles. Adjust pattern if necessary.

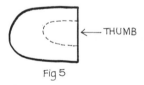

Fig 5

Thumb pocket on lower mouth The human thumb is too small to be used as a lower mouth on its own. In all the puppets the lower mouth is made to a size that looks natural. Then part of it is stitched to form a pocket to enclose the thumb. By this means when the thumb moves the whole lower mouth moves with it; up and down or, in some models, twisted to show other emotions. Without a thumb pocket the thumb would move inside the mouth but the

20

mouth itself would remain stationary. Test width and length of thumb pocket for your thumb, but pass reasonable sideways ease. Thumb pocket is in centre of mouth so that puppet can be operated on right or left hand.

Beak or Mouth into Body

In the following instructions the word 'beak' means 'beak' or 'mouth' depending on which puppet is being made. On fur fabric clip off fur pile for $\frac{1}{4}$ in (6 mm) round AC on body and lower beak to make parts less bulky for sewing.

Mark, with thread or tailor's chalk, points A and C at centre and side of mouth hole on body. Body is wrong side out, beak right side out. Hold beak and slip it through the mouth hole in body, like posting a letter. Slip the tip of the beak in first and upper beak should be on top. Push it through till beak is on right side of body and line AA matches points A on body.

Fig 6

Fig. 6 shows beak slotted through front body for Crow, Owl and Penguin.

Fig 7

Fig 7 shows beak or mouth dotted between the two bodies for Cock-a-Doodle-Doo, Dog, Kangaroo and Rabbit.

22

Still working on wrong side of body pin edges of beak and body together, matching points A at sides, point C at centre of upper beak to C at top of mouth hole and point C at centre of lower beak to C at bottom of mouth hole. Slip in hand and check that you have not pinned across any of the openings. Backstitch right round mouth hole using double thread of body colour. Raw edges of beak and of mouth hole are on wrong side of body.

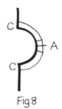

Fig 8

Fig. 8 Slit the seam allowance at A on each side. Oversew edges all round opening to prevent fraying as this part receives a lot of wear. Turn to right side.

Puppets

Peter Penguin, Hoolet the Owl and Croaky Crow

Croaky Crow 18 in (45·7 cm) high, Hoolet the Owl—Hoolet is the old Scottish word for an owl—16 in (40·6 cm) high and Peter Penguin 22 in (55·9 cm) high are all variations of the same pattern. In all of them puppeteer's arm enters at back of head.

Peter Penguin is the comedian. He comes complete with a supply of small fish which can be tossed to him to catch, or can be fed to him. He will gobble them up and they disappear down inside him.

MATERIALS

CROAKY CROW

$\frac{3}{4}$ yd (60 cm) black satin, $\frac{1}{4}$ yd (30 cm) orange fabric and 6 in (20 cm) thin fabric of any colour for pad, all at 36 in (90 cm) wide; $\frac{1}{4}$ yd (30 cm) interlining for stiffening; 2 joggle eyes; stuffing; thread in black and orange.

HOOLET THE OWL

$\frac{1}{2}$ yd (50 cm) brown and black patterned fabric, $\frac{1}{4}$ yd (30 cm) turquoise blue fabric and 6 in (20 cm) thin fabric of any colour for pad, all at 36 in (90 cm) wide; yellow fabric 7 in (17·8 cm) square; $\frac{1}{4}$ yd (30 cm) interlining for stiffening; 2 joggle eyes; stuffing; thread in brown, turquoise and yellow.

PETER PENGUIN

$\frac{3}{4}$ yd (60 cm) black satin, $\frac{1}{4}$ yd (30 cm) orange fabric and 6 in (20 cm) thin fabric of any colour for pad, all at 36 in (90 cm) wide; white satin, $16\frac{3}{4}$ in × 6 in (42·5 cm × 15·3 cm); $\frac{1}{4}$ yd (30 cm) interlining for stiffening; glitter fabric $6\frac{1}{2}$ in × 4 in (16·5 cm × 10·2 cm) for each fish required; 2 joggle eyes; stuffing; thread in black, white, orange and to match fish.

PATTERNS

Make paper patterns from squared diagrams as described on page 13. Base of body, wings and tail are cut full size for fabric and $\frac{1}{4}$ in (6 mm) smaller all round for stiffening. Thumb pocket and mouth hole patterns are in paper only.

CROAKY CROW

Black fabric Cut one front body, two back bodies reversing pattern to make a pair, one base of body, four wings and two tails. *Orange fabric* One inner beak, one upper beak, one lower beak and four feet. Cut two rectangles, each 4 in × 2 in (10·2 cm × 5·1 cm) for legs. *Pad fabric* Two head pads and one base of head pad. *Stiffening* One base of body, two wings and one tail.

HOOLET THE OWL

Brown patterned cotton Cut one front body, two back bodies reversing pattern to make a pair, one base of body and four wings. *Turquoise blue fabric* One inner beak, one upper beak, one lower beak, one beak extension and four feet. *Yellow fabric* Four circles, each $3\frac{1}{2}$ in (8·9 cm) in diameter. *Pad fabric* Two head pads and one base of head pad. *Stiffening* One base of body, two wings and two circles each 3 in (7·6 cm) in diameter.

PETER PENGUIN

Black fabric Cut one front body, two back bodies reversing pattern to make a pair, one base of body and four wings. *White fabric* One white front. *Orange fabric* One inner beak, one upper beak, one lower beak and four feet. *Pad fabric* Two head pads and one base of head pad. *Stiffening* One base of body and two wings. *Glitter fabric* Two sides for each fish, reversing pattern to make a pair.

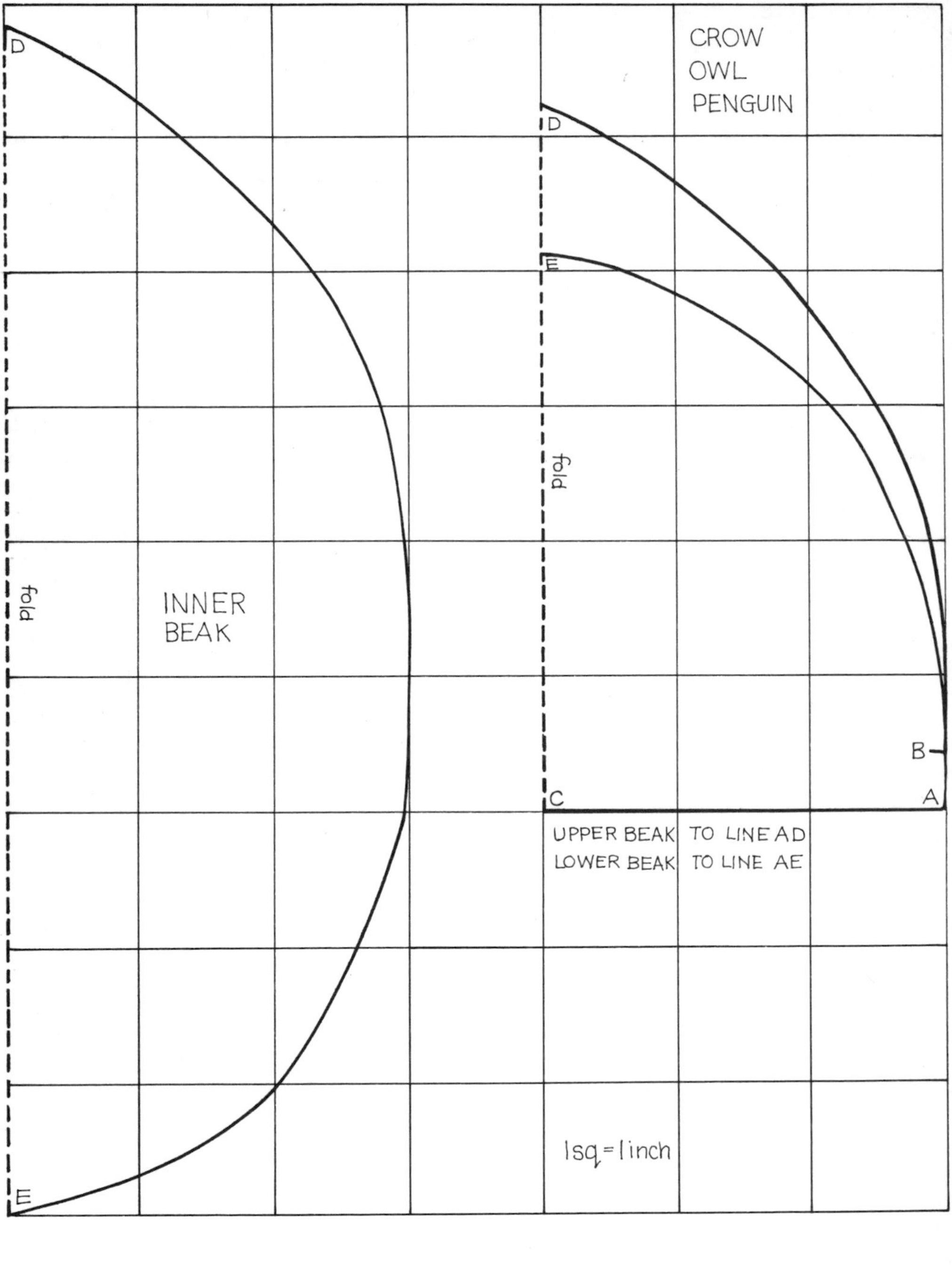

CROW
OWL
PENGUIN

D

E

fold

fold

INNER
BEAK

B

C   A

UPPER BEAK | TO LINE AD
LOWER BEAK | TO LINE AE

D

E

1 sq = 1 inch

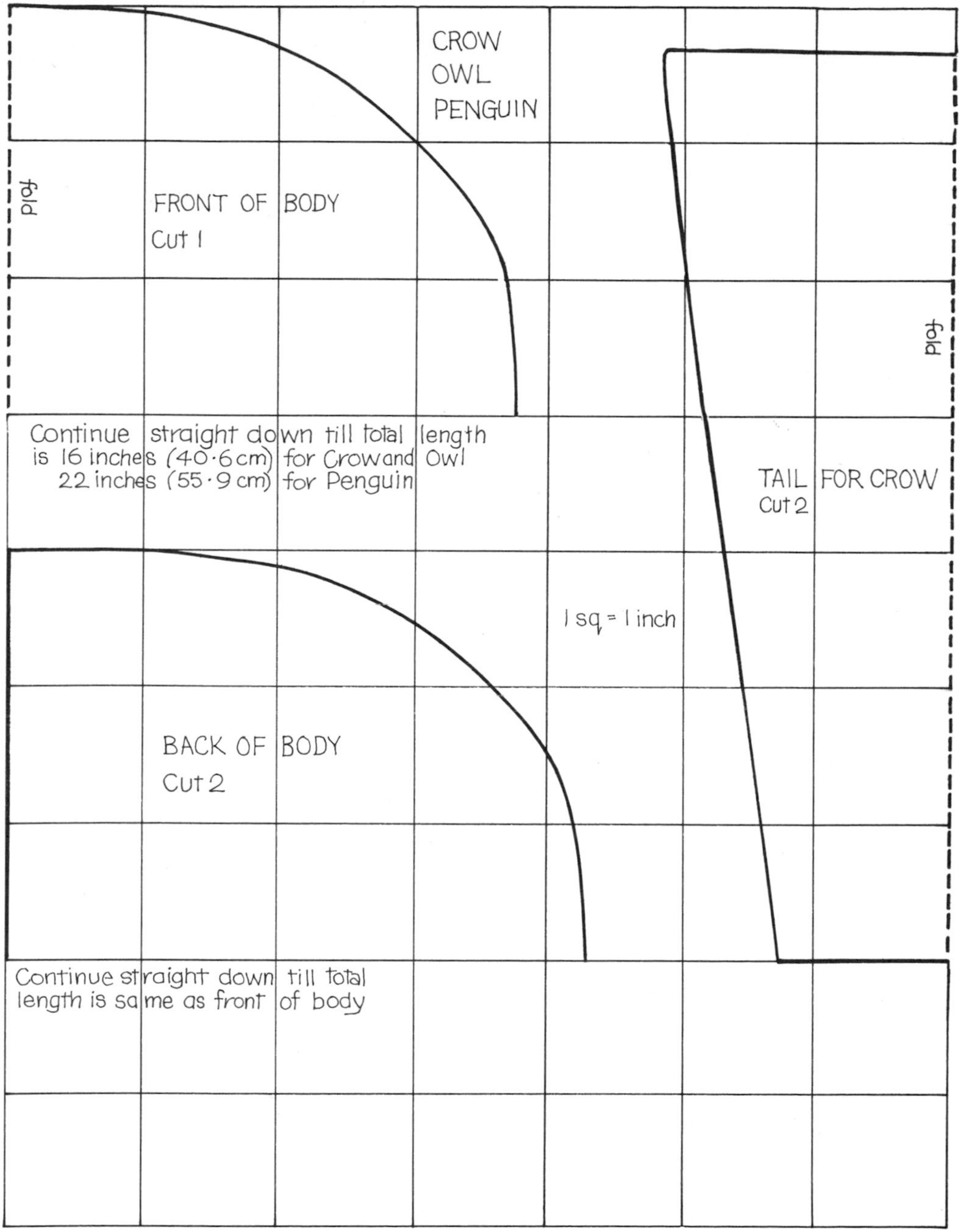

CROW
OWL
PENGUIN

fold

FRONT OF BODY
Cut 1

fold

Continue straight down till total length
is 16 inches (40·6 cm) for Crow and Owl
22 inches (55·9 cm) for Penguin

TAIL FOR CROW
Cut 2

1 sq = 1 inch

BACK OF BODY
Cut 2

Continue straight down till total
length is same as front of body

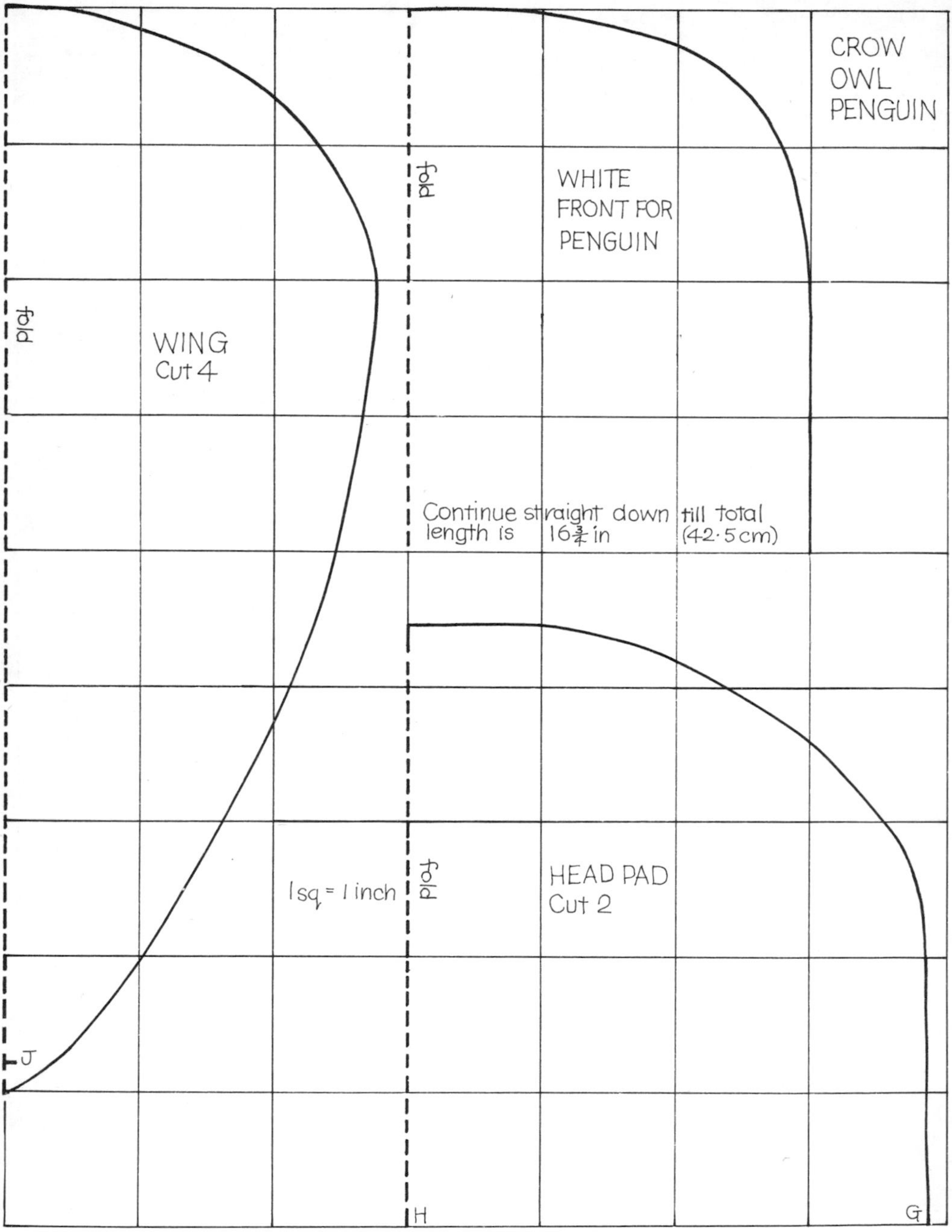

CROW
OWL
PENGUIN

fold

WHITE
FRONT FOR
PENGUIN

fold

WING
Cut 4

Continue straight down till total
length is 16¾ in (42·5 cm)

1 sq = 1 inch

fold

HEAD PAD
Cut 2

J

H

G

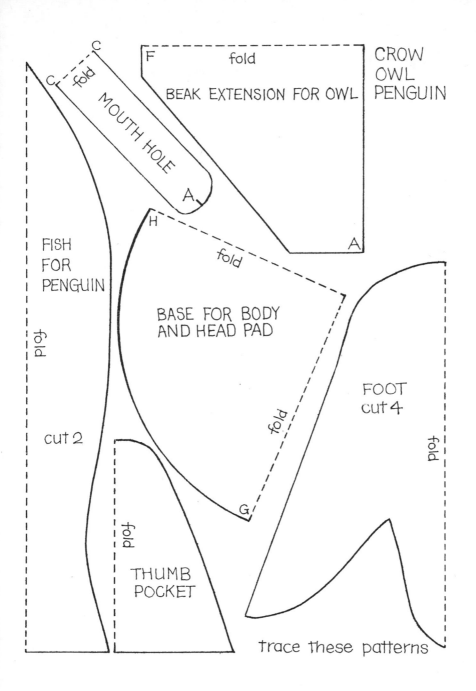

C
fold
C

F
fold
BEAK EXTENSION FOR OWL

CROW
OWL
PENGUIN

MOUTH HOLE

A

H
fold
A

FISH
FOR
PENGUIN

fold

BASE FOR BODY
AND HEAD PAD

fold

FOOT
cut 4

fold

cut 2

fold

G

THUMB
POCKET

trace these patterns

All backstitch is done $\frac{1}{4}$ in (6 mm) from edge, unless otherwise stated.

BEAK

(Crow, Owl, Penguin) Follow standard instructions, page 19.

Fig 1   Fig 2

BEAK INTO BODY

(Crow, Owl, Penguin) Work on front body, wrong side upwards.

Fig. 1 Measure $4\frac{1}{2}$ in (11·4 cm) from centre top, shown by dotted line, and pin on mouth hole pattern. Cut round it to cut out mouth hole. Now turn to page 22 and follow standard instructions for Beak or Mouth into Body.

Fig. 2 (Crow and Penguin) Sew eyes to head, using thread double. Centre of eye is about $1\frac{1}{2}$ in (3·8 cm) above mouth.

BEAK EXTENSION (Owl only)

Fig. 3 Slit $\frac{1}{4}$ in (6 mm) from centre top shown as dotted line from F. Turn edge AA to wrong side and tack down. Turn each side from F to A to wrong side and tack down. The top slit makes this easy.
    Pin to body, line AA touching top of beak. Using turquoise thread

34

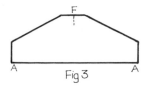

Fig 3

ladder stitch along AA, hem other sides. While sewing keep finger inside bill to make sure opening is not closed.

BEAK FEEDING HOLE (Penguin only)

Feeding hole pattern
Fig 4

open beak

Right hand Fig 5 left hand

Fig. 4 Trace pattern and cut out in paper.

Fig. 5 Lay penguin flat and open beak wide. Thumb pocket is shown dotted. Pin pattern of hole between thumb pocket and edge of mouth, but lying on upper beak. The first drawing shows the position for a right-handed puppeteer and the second drawing for a left-handed puppeteer. Placed like this fish will slide through hole into hollow of hand and drop down inside penguin's body.

Cut out hole, only cutting through inner mouth. Blanket stitch edge of hole in orange thread to prevent fraying.

WHITE FRONT (Penguin only)

Turn all edges $\frac{1}{2}$ in (1·2 cm) to wrong side. Round the top fold curves as necessary to make fabric lie flat. Tack and press to get a crisp edge. Pin to front of body with base line just over $\frac{1}{4}$ in (6 mm) from foot. Sew down. Least conspicuous method is small hem stitches with white thread but quickest method is to machine, in white, close to edge.

BACK OF BODY (Crow, Owl and Penguin)

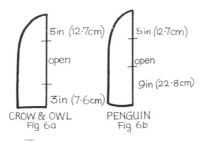

CROW & OWL
Fig 6a

PENGUIN
Fig 6b

Fig. 6a and 6b Pin two backs of body together, wrong sides to outside. Backstitch on straight side, $\frac{1}{2}$ in (1·2 cm) from edge, leaving opening as shown. Round opening turn edge twice to wrong side and hem.

Open out to form one back, with opening for puppeteer's hand in centre. Pin back and front bodies together, wrong sides to outside. Backstitch round outer edge, leaving base open. Mark centre of front body at base. This will be point H.

TAIL (Crow only)

Tack stiffener to wrong side of one tail. Pin other tail to it, wrong sides to outside. Backstitch, leaving short end open. Oversew edges round opening to prevent fraying. Turn to right side and remove tacking.

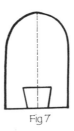

Fig 7

36

Fig. 7 Turn body to right side. Tack tail to back of body so that open end lies on base.

LEGS (Crow only)

Fold each leg in half lengthwise, wrong side to outside. Backstitch leg on one short side and one long side. Turn edges of opening to wrong side and tack down. Turn to right side.

Fig 8

Fig. 8 Tack each leg to front of body so that the short ends that are sewn lie on base. Place each leg about halfway between centre point and side seam. Turn body to wrong side.

BASE OF BODY (Crow, Owl, Penguin)

Fig. 9 On base stiffener mark points G and H. Pin on wrong side of fabric base and use thread the colour of fabric to catch down at each of these points. Pin base into foot of body, wrong sides to outside.

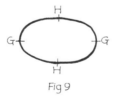

Fig 9

Points G should match side seams, with points H at centre of front body and main seam of back body. Backstitch, using thread double, round edge. Turn body to right side.

Fig. 10 On Crow legs and tail will all be firmly attached to body.

Fig 10

HEAD PAD (Crow, Owl, Penguin)

Fig. 11 Pin two head pads together, wrong sides to outside. Backstitch sides, leaving top and base open. Pin base into open end of head pad, matching points G and H. Backstitch round edge. Turn edge of top opening to wrong side and tack down. Turn pad to right side. Stuff pad, working with base on table to keep it flat. Keep sides well rounded, but do not overstuff pad. If overstuffed, pad will sag down and impede puppeteer's hand. Ladder stitch to close opening.

Fig 11

Slip pad through back of puppet into top of head. Side seams of pad match side seams of puppet. Make sure top of pad is fully into top of head. To fix pad in place sew jutting-out seam allowance of upper mouth where it joins body to line G to G at base of pad. Fold back puppet's body to see where you are working. These stitches will not show so can be large. Use thread double. Pull back puppet body. Put hand into mouth and check that opening has not been closed. Take a few stitches to attach centre back of pad, point H, to centre back seam of body. To help prevent pad sagging down, press upwards and stitch at that point using thread to match fabric.

38

FEET (Crow, Owl, Penguin)

Fig. 12 Pin two feet together, wrong sides to outside. Backstitch right round foot, leaving top open. Turn edges of opening to wrong side and tack down. Snip surplus fabric between toes and at tip, shown dotted on fig. 12. Turn feet to right side. Stuff, doing tip of each toe with small bits of stuffing then rest of foot. Ladder stitch to close opening.

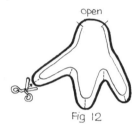

Fig 12

Fig 13

Fig. 13 (Owl and Penguin) Hold puppet upside down. Sew feet to base of body. Use thread double, of colour of foot, and hem or ladder stitch round back of foot to base, then ladder stitch across between front of foot and base to keep foot from sagging down.

(Crow) Push stuffing up each leg a little at a time. Leave open at end. Sew a foot to open end of each leg. Hold puppet upside down and use thread double to ladder stitch round twice. If foot hangs down do another row of ladder stitch along front of leg taking up more of the fabric.

WINGS (Crow, Owl, Penguin)

Fig. 14 Tack stiffeners to wrong side of two wings. Use thread of fabric colour to catch tip of stiffener to fabric at J. These stitches will stay in. Pin other two wings to stiffened ones, wrong sides to outside. Backstitch, leaving opening, as shown. Turn edges of opening to wrong side and tack down, then snip surplus fabric from J to edge, shown by dotted line on fig. 14. Turn to right side. Remove tacking.

39

Fig 14

Fig 15

Fig. 15 Sew a wing to each side of body. Centre top of wing is sewn to side seam, about 2 in (5·1 cm) lower than mouth. Oversew using thread double. Keep stitches to centre top so that wing is secure yet loose enough to flap as puppet moves.

Croaky Crow is now finished.

EYES (Owl only)

For each eye tack a stiffener circle to wrong side of one yellow circle. On right side of second yellow circle put pencil mark in exact centre. Pin the two circles together wrong sides to outside.

Backstitch $\frac{1}{4}$ in (6 mm) from edge leaving opening. Round opening turn edges to wrong side and tack down. Turn to right side. Ladder stitch to close opening. Press to get crisp edge.

Fig 16

Fig. 16 Using thread double sew joggle eye to mark made in centre of eye. Ladder stitch eyes to owl. Lower edge of yellow circles to just touch top of beak. Yellow circles overlap beak extension which is shown striped. With care stitches can be made on under side of yellow circle leaving top fabric with its crisply pressed outline.

Hoolet the Owl is now finished.

40

FISH (Penguin only)

Fig. 17 Pin two fish together wrong sides to outside. Backstitch leaving opening on lower side. Round opening turn edges to wrong side and tack down. Turn to right side. Stuff lightly; if too well stuffed fish might not slip through feeding hole in mouth. Ladder stitch to close hole. Using black thread double, sew straight stitches to form an eye on each side of head.

Fig 17

Make a number of fish. Peter Penguin can eat at least six consecutively.

FEEDING PETER PENGUIN

Fig. 18 Play with the penguin and the fish. Have fish in a small basket. Toss up a fish with the free hand, catching it crossways in the penguin's beak. Penguin can dislike fish and toss it back to be caught in the puppeteer's free hand.

Fig 18

Fig 19

Fig. 19 To feed the penguin the fish has to be guided, head first, into its mouth. Hold the fish by the tail and offer it to the penguin.

The penguin tilts its head up in the air and opens its mouth. Guide the fish's head slowly into the feeding hole and let the penguin make gurgling sounds as it begins to disappear. When the fish is about half eaten the hand inside the bill can do a little jerking to let the penguin devour the rest of the fish unaided.

The fish drops down into the base of the penguin's body where it can lie out of sight for the rest of the entertainment.

Peter Penguin is now finished.

Cock-a-Doodle-Doo

Cock-a-Doodle-Doo is a glamorous puppet, made in yellow fur fabric with a magnificent tail of golden tinsel, such as is used for Christmas decorations. The puppeteer's hand enters underneath the body and goes up through body and neck.

He measures 27 in (68·5 cm) in height and 26 in (66 cm) from beak to tail.

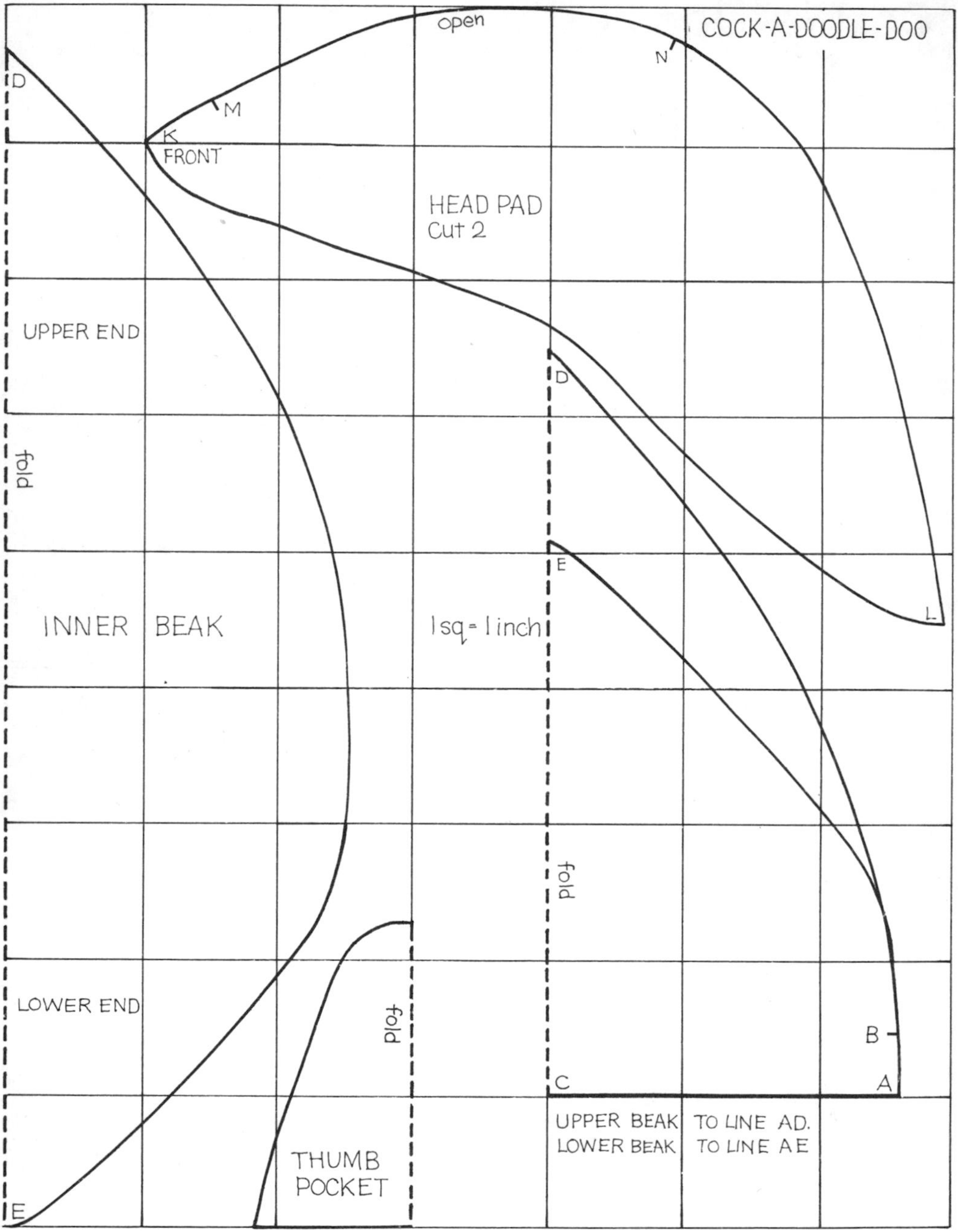

COCK·A·DOODLE·DOO

open

N

M

K FRONT

D

HEAD PAD
Cut 2

UPPER END

fold

D

E

INNER BEAK

1 sq = 1 inch

L

LOWER END

fold

fold

B

C

A

UPPER BEAK | TO LINE AD.
LOWER BEAK | TO LINE AE

THUMB
POCKET

E

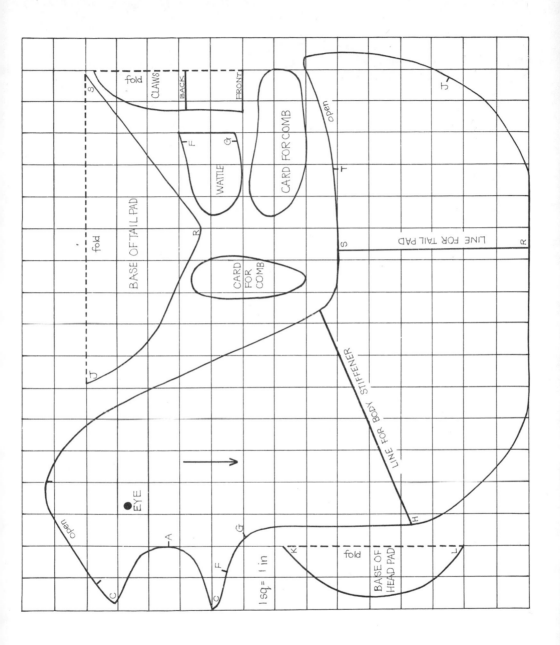

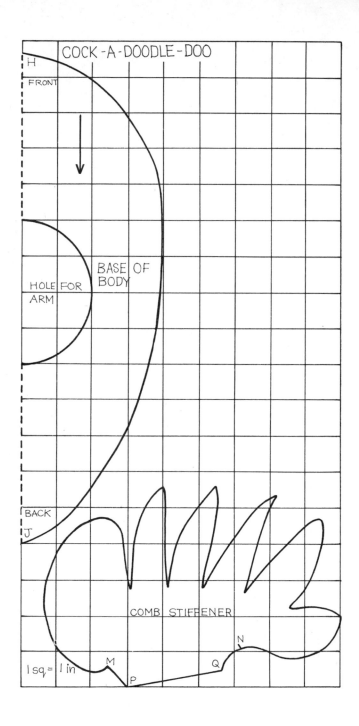

COCK-A-DOODLE-DOO

H

FRONT

HOLE FOR
ARM

BASE OF
BODY

BACK

J

COMB STIFFENER

1 sq. = 1 in

M

P

Q

N

MATERIALS

½ yd (40 cm) yellow fur fabric, ½ yd (40 cm) orange fabric, ¼ yd (20 cm) red fabric, ¼ yd (20 cm) thin fabric any colour for pads, all at 36 in (90 cm) wide; 1 yd (80 cm) interlining for stiffening; gold tinsel, two strands each 36 in (90 cm) long; pieces of stiff card; 12 in (30·5 cm) dowel rod of ½ in (1·2 cm) diameter; 2 joggle eyes; stuffing and thread in yellow, orange and red.

PATTERNS

Make paper patterns from squared diagrams as described at front of book. Make patterns for tail pad and body stiffener by drawing extra body patterns and cutting them from tail to lines shown, see figs. 1 and 2. Thumb pocket is in paper only. Arrows on patterns show direction in which fur fabric should stroke.

Yellow fur fabric Cut two bodies, reversing pattern to make a pair, and one base of body. Hole for arm in centre of base is a circle, 4 in (10·2 cm) in diameter. Instead of drafting out curve on pattern, just mark its position, cut a paper circle and trace it to make the hole. Fig 3 shows economical layout for ½ yd (40 cm) of 36 in (90 cm) fabric, laying base across the pile. If more fabric is available lay base following arrow on pattern.

Fig 1 Fig 2 Fig 3

Orange fabric One inner beak, one upper beak, one lower beak, two pieces each 12 in × 4 in (30·5 cm × 10·2 cm) for legs, one piece 13 in × 2 in (33 cm × 5·1 cm) to cover stick, two circles each 1½ in (3·8 cm) in diameter, six front claws cut full length of claws pattern

47

and two back claws cut to shorter line. *Red fabric* Two wattles, reversing pattern to make a pair, and two pieces each 9 in × 6 in (22·8 cm × 15·3 cm) for comb. *Pad fabric* Two tail pads, see fig. 1, one base of tail pad, two head pads and one base of head pad. *Stiffening* Two body stiffeners, as fig. 2, one base of body and one comb stiffener, all in interlining. One each of the two 'Card for comb' patterns in stiff card.

SEWING

All backstitch is done ¼ in (6 mm) from edge.

BEAK

Follow standard instructions, page 19.

WATTLE

Pin two wattles together, wrong sides to outside. Backstitch round outer edge, leaving FG open. Turn to right side and press.

BODY

Use thread on right side of each body to mark position of eye. Tack stiffener to each side of body and to base of body, all on wrong side. Blanket-stitch round hole for arm in base of body to hold fabric and stiffener together and neaten edge. Using thread double, sew on eyes.

Fig. 4 Tack wattle to right side of one body, matching points F and G.

Fig 4   Fig 5

Fig. 5 Pin two bodies together and pin base between bodies matching points H and J, all wrong sides to outside. Using thread double backstitch sides of body together leaving openings between points C at mouth, on top of head and at tail. Then backstitch right round base of body. Round head and tail openings turn edges to wrong side and tack down.

BEAK INTO BODY

Turn to page 22 and follow standard instructions for Beak or Mouth into Body. Wattle will appear, firmly held in place below head, when puppet is turned to right side.

COMB AND HEAD PAD

Pin two head pads together, wrong sides to outside. Backstitch K to M and N to L. Round opening between M and N turn edges to wrong side and tack down. Backstitch base of head pad between points K and L, sewing right round base. Turn to right side. Stuff lightly, rounding out sides but not letting base sag down. Ladder stitch to close opening.

Fig. 6 Pin two pieces of red fabric together, wrong sides outside. Tack interlining comb stiffener to fabric. Backstitch round top of comb, on stiffening, as close to edge as possible, from M to N, leaving MPQN open. Cut out red fabric, about $\frac{1}{4}$ in (6 mm) from edge all round. Between points of comb cut straight down to edge of stiffening. Turn to right side. This is tricky but turn out one narrow part at a time—a stuffing stick or knitting needle helps. Press.

Fig 6

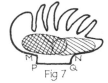

Fig 7

Fig. 7 Push the small card stiffener into the end point of the comb, shown shaded. Then push the large card stiffener into the front end of the comb, shown with crossed lines. The two will overlap. Stitch across from M to N to hold the cards in place.

Fig. 8 Open out fabric on comb from M to P and from N to Q to form two flaps. Pin one flap to each side of head pad, matching points M and N. Sew round MPQN on each side of head pad. Comb now sits firmly on top of head pad.

Fig. 9 Slip end of head pad, L, through opening in top of head. Adjust head pad until comb, from points M and N, juts out of head. Pad is shown dotted inside head. Put hand up from hole for arm in base of body and press head pad into the curve of the head. Pin edges of opening on head to sides of comb. Using yellow thread double, close head opening by stitching from side to side through comb along line M to N. This closes head opening, fixes comb in place and holds up head pad. Give extra support at end of head pad at L or close to it. Use yellow thread double, press up end of pad with one hand inside body, and take two stitches on outside of body on neck seam, stitching through fur fabric to pad. Stitches will be lost in the pile of the fabric.

When puppet is finished examine comb again. If comb is flopping sideways ladder stitch between comb and head, on side opposite to one that is sagging, to pull it upright. Use yellow thread.

LEGS AND FEET

Fold each leg piece in half lengthwise, wrong sides to outside.

50

Backstitch long edge. Backstitch one of the circles into one end of leg. This will be the foot end. At top of leg turn edge to wrong side. Tack down. Turn leg to right side. Stuff and leave top open.

Fold each claw in half, wrong side to outside. Backstitch long side. At open end turn edge to wrong side. Tack down. Turn to right side and stuff, leaving end open.

Fig. 10 Sew claws to end of leg. Folded side of claw lies on ground. Seam of leg is to back. The short back claw is sewn to seam of leg. One front claw to centre front of leg with another front claw each side of it. Use thread double and ladder-stitch twice round open end of claws.

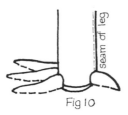

Fig 10

Sew open top of each leg to base of body. One leg goes on each side of hole for arm. Use thread double and ladder stitch round twice.

TAIL

Cover stick with strip of orange fabric. On wrong side gather each short end $\frac{1}{4}$ in (6 mm) from edge. Pull up tight and finish off thread. Turn one long side $\frac{1}{4}$ in (6 mm) to wrong side. Tack down with short stitches which can be left in. Turn to right side. Fold round stick, tucking in the long unfinished side and folding the tacked side over it. Hem down.

Fig. 11 Pin two tail pads together, wrong sides to outside. Pin base of tail pad between the two tail pads matching points J, R and S. Backstitch sides of tail pad, from J to tip of tail and from S to T, then

Fig 11

Fig 12

backstitch right round base. Round opening turn edges to wrong side and tack down. Turn to right side.

Fig. 12 Stuff pad and when nearly finished push in covered stick. Keep it close to the tip of the tail and push it right down to the base. Finish stuffing round it. Oversew across stuffing hole to close it and ladder stitch stick to each side of pad fabric.

Fig. 13 Put pad into body. Slip it in through hole in base putting stick in first and up through opening at tail. Dots on fig. 13 show pad inside body. Using yellow thread double, ladder stitch sides of opening at tail and sew the fur fabric firmly to each side of stick. Fix base of tail pad by sewing point R to edge of hole for arm. Sew for about one inch (2·5 cm) where they meet.

Fig 13

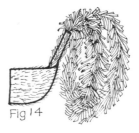

Fig 14

Fig. 14 Fold each strand of tinsel in half, giving four thicknesses in all. The cut ends are placed touching the body. The strands are sewn along the stick then fly loose in two big loops. Use orange thread double. Sew one strand at a time, sewing over the central core of the tinsel and through the fabric on the stick. Pull out the short spikes of tinsel as stitch is being tightened. This keeps the upright part of the tail very fluffy and disguises the stick and the sewing.

 Check that tinsel is hanging to back of puppet. A few stitches on the top of the stick can keep the tinsel lying in the correct direction.

Slimy Snail

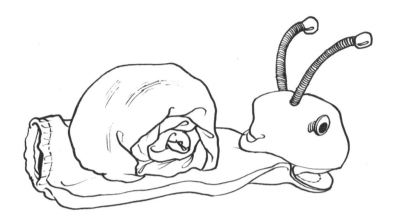

Slimy Snail is one of the simplest puppets in the book. He is long and slinky in red fabric with a silver grey shell. His eyes stand out on stalks and he has long horns. He is 17 in (43 cm) long. The puppeteer's arm goes in the end of the body and Slimy lies horizontally from fingers to elbow.

MATERIALS

½ yd (50 cm) red fabric, ¾ yd (60 cm) silver grey fabric, ¼ yd (20 cm) thin fabric any colour for pad, all at 36 in (90 cm) wide; piece of stiff card 7 in × 5 in (17·8 cm × 12·7 cm); approx. 11 in (27·9 cm) elastic; small balls of red and black wool; 2 joggle eyes; stuffing and thread in red and silver grey.

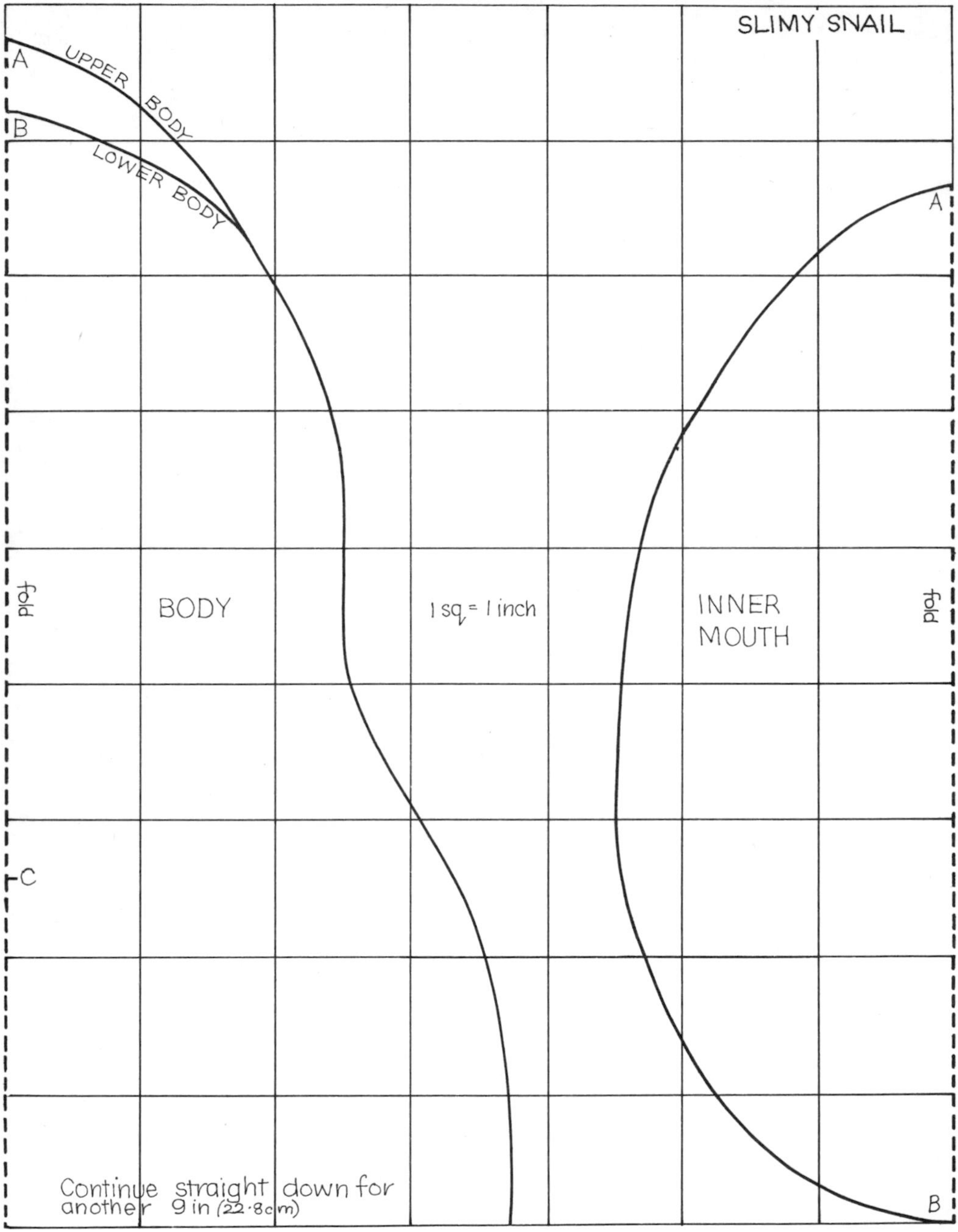

SLIMY SNAIL

A

UPPER BODY

B

LOWER BODY

A

fold

BODY

1 sq = 1 inch

INNER
MOUTH

fold

C

B

Continue straight down for
another 9 in (22.8cm)

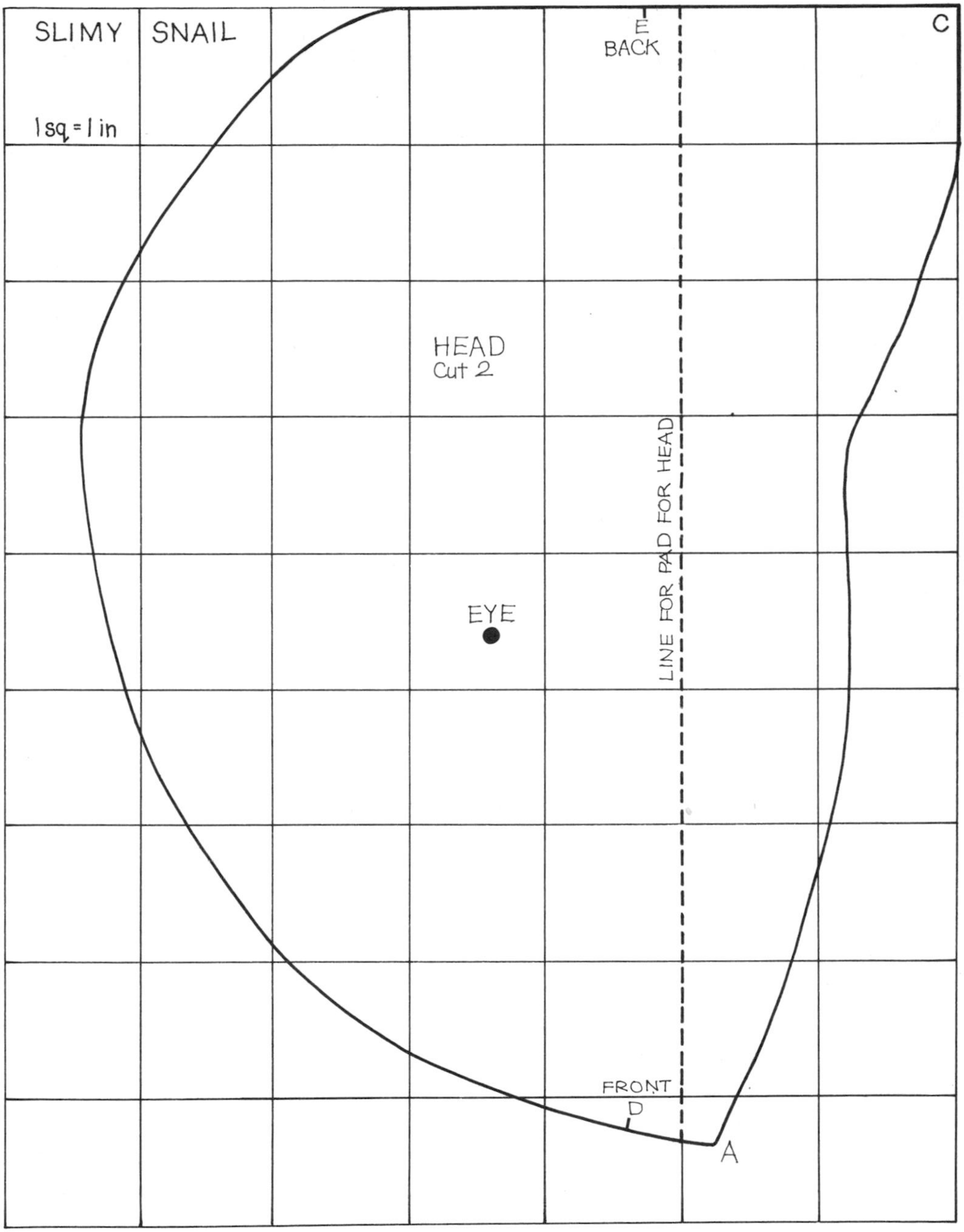

SLIMY SNAIL

1 sq = 1 in

HEAD
Cut 2

EYE
●

E
BACK

C

LINE FOR PAD FOR HEAD

FRONT
D

A

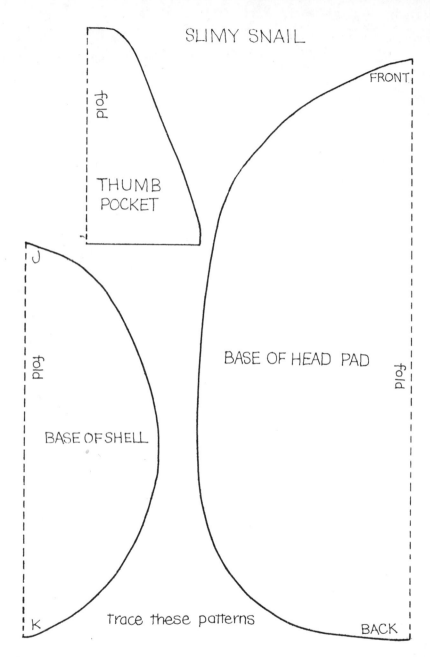

SLIMY SNAIL

THUMB POCKET

FRONT

fold

BASE OF HEAD PAD

fold

J

BASE OF SHELL

fold

K

Trace these patterns

BACK

PATTERNS

Make paper patterns from squared diagrams as described at front of book. Thumb pocket is in paper only.

Red fabric Cut two bodies, cutting upper body to point A and lower body to point B, one inner mouth, two heads cutting to full size of pattern and reversing pattern to make a pair, two pieces each 2 in × 1¼ in (5·1 cm × 3·2 cm) for eye stalks and two pieces each 12 in × 1¼ in (30·5 cm × 3·2 cm) for horns. *Silver grey fabric* Two pieces each 32 in × 10 in (81·3 cm × 25·4 cm) and one base of shell. *Pad fabric* Two head pads, cutting head pattern from top to dotted line, and one base of head pad. *Card* Cut upper body pattern as far as point C.

SEWING

All backstitch is done ¼ in (6 mm) from edge.

BODY

Use thread to mark point C on right side of upper body.

Fig. 1 Pin inner mouth between the two ends of the bodies, matching points A and B. All have wrong sides to outside. Backstitch right round inner mouth. Backstitch side seams of bodies together. At open end turn edge over to wrong side as little as possible. Tack down. Turn over again for ½ in (1·2 cm). Backstitch close to edge, leaving a gap at each side seam.

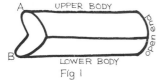

Fig 1

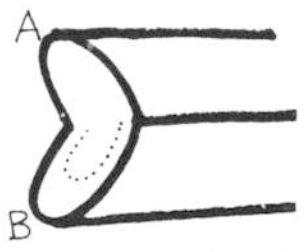

Fig 2

Fig. 2 Turn body to right side. Open mouth and pin thumb pocket pattern on inside of lower mouth. Open end of thumb pocket lies

57

about $\frac{1}{2}$ in (1·2 cm) from junction of upper and lower mouths. Sew small running stitches round the edge of the pattern, going through both thicknesses of lower mouth and of lower body. Leave straight edge open.

Thread elastic through the hem at open end of puppet. Length is approximate as body should grip puppeteer's arm fairly tightly to give good control of mouth. Put safety pin on end of elastic. Start threading at one seam hole. Hole at second seam is to help to guide elastic through that part. Carry on to starting point. Sew ends of elastic together very firmly. Test puppet over type of sleeve likely to be worn. Alter elastic if necessary. When correct sew down gaps at seams.

HEAD

Use thread to mark point for eye on right side of each head.

Fig 3   Fig 4

Figs. 3 and 4 Pin two heads together and two head pads together, all wrong sides to outside. Backstitch heads from A over the top to C and head pads over the top. Round open end of head, AC, turn edge $\frac{1}{4}$ in (6 mm) to wrong side and tack down. Turn head to right side. Pin base of head pad into open end of head pad, matching front and back points. Backstitch round edge, leaving opening for stuffing in one side. Turn edge of opening to wrong side and tack down. Turn to right side. Stuff pad, trying to keep base flat. Ladder stitch to close opening.

Hold head upside down and slip head pad into it, front to point D, back to point E. Make sure that curved top of pad fits properly into curved top of head. When satisfied with fit use red thread double and sew pad to inside of head at D and E. Stitch on the seam allowance of the head and stitches will not show on outside.

58

HEAD TO BODY

Trim the sides of the card until it fits neatly into upper mouth. It lets you pin and sew without fear of closing mouth and gives some solidity for the sewing.

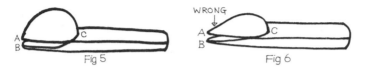

Fig. 5 Pin the head to the top of the body. Match points C first at back of head and on body. Then pin point A. Head looks its best if sitting straight up from point A and not sagging back as shown by arrow in fig. 6. Fingers in finger pocket need room so make sure that head pad is not pressing down onto mouth. Pin sides of head along edge of upper mouth from A, then across top of body to point C. Using thread double ladder stitch right round head. Remove card.

EYES AND HORNS

Tack the pieces of red fabric for each eye stalk and for each horn with red thread and leave it in.

Eyes Fold each short edge $\frac{1}{4}$ in (6 mm) to wrong side. Tack down. Now fold each long edge to centre of wrong side and tack down.

Fold in half lengthwise so that right side is to outside and all edges are enclosed; then catch outside edges together. Now fold in half from top to bottom and catch at bottom.

Fig 7

Use red wool to bind each eye stalk tightly. Lay end of wool along stalk, then start winding as close to folded top as possible. Keep layers of wool touching till as near bottom end as possible. Break wool, leaving a few inches or centimetres. Thread needle and sew end of wool under or through stalk to finish it off.

Sew an eye to the top of each eye stalk, using red thread double. Sew bottom of each stalk to head on mark for eye. Ladder stitch round at least twice till stalk and eye feel really secure, sewing into pad as well as top fabric. Eye sticks straight out from side of head.

Horns Use black wool to bind each horn tightly. Use same method as eye stalk, but begin lower down leaving about $\frac{1}{2}$ in (1·2 cm) of red stalk showing as a red tip to the horn.

Sew bottom end of each horn to head, as eye stalk. Sew horn higher up and further back on head.

Home-made eyes If home-made eyes are preferred make the eye $\frac{1}{2}$ in (1·2 cm) larger in diameter than needed. Cut circle of red fabric to this size for backing. Backstitch eye and backing together on wrong side, leaving an opening. Turn to right side, stuff and close opening. This will give a solid eye for sewing to the eye stalk.

SHELL

Fig. 8 Fold silver grey fabric in half, wrong side to outside. Backstitch long edges together, leaving opening in middle for stuffing and leaving both ends open. Round opening for stuffing turn edge $\frac{1}{4}$ in (6 mm) to wrong side and tack down.

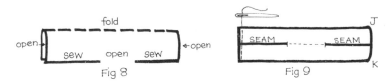

Fig 8   Fig 9

Fig. 9 Refold shell so that seam comes in centre of one side. Backstitch across one short end. At other short end pin in base of shell matching points J and K. Backstitch right round base. Turn shell to right side. Stuff lightly. Shell will be broad at base end but reduce stuffing till shell is fairly shallow at other end. Ladder stitch to close stuffing hole.

Fig. 10 Coil shell, starting at shallow end. At the first bend ladder stitch right across shell to hold shallow end from uncoiling.

Fig 10

Fig 11

Fig. 11 Continue coiling fairly tightly. At base end ladder stitch across shell again to hold last coil in place. To give extra stability ladder stitch round the coils of the shell on the outer edge on each side. Sew slightly into the coil so that outer edge does not appear to be sewn.

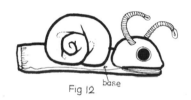

Fig 12

base

Fig. 12 Slip folded magazine into puppet to keep body sides apart for stitching. Mark a point about 2 in (5·1 cm) from end of head. Place base of shell on this mark. Using red thread double ladder stitch twice round foot of shell. Take big stitches on first round to balance shell in position. Remove magazine. Put puppet on arm and check that mouth opens properly. When mouth opens wide head tilts back. If shell is too close to head it will obstruct the head. If satisfactory put in magazine again and do second round of ladder stitch.

Dandy Dog

Dandy Dog is made in fur fabric. The puppeteer's hand enters at the centre back of the body. He can stand and hold the dog upright or the dog can sit on his knee. Dandy Dog is 28 in (71 cm) high.

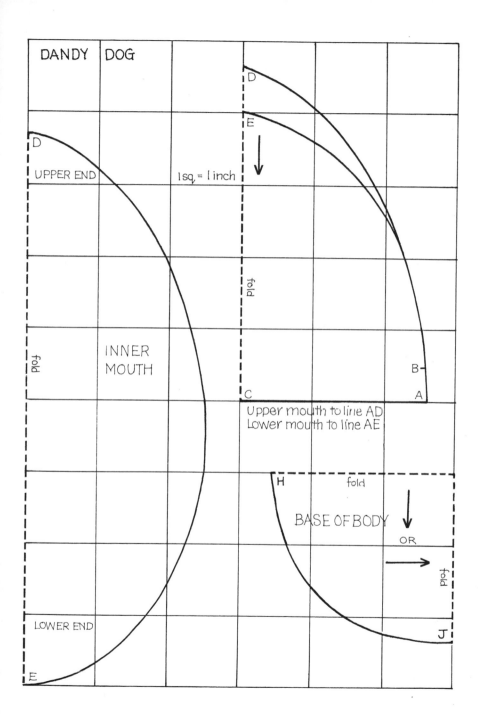

DANDY DOG

UPPER END

1 sq. = 1 inch

fold

INNER MOUTH

fold

Upper mouth to line AD
Lower mouth to line AE

D

E

B

C

A

fold

BASE OF BODY

OR

fold

LOWER END

E

H

J

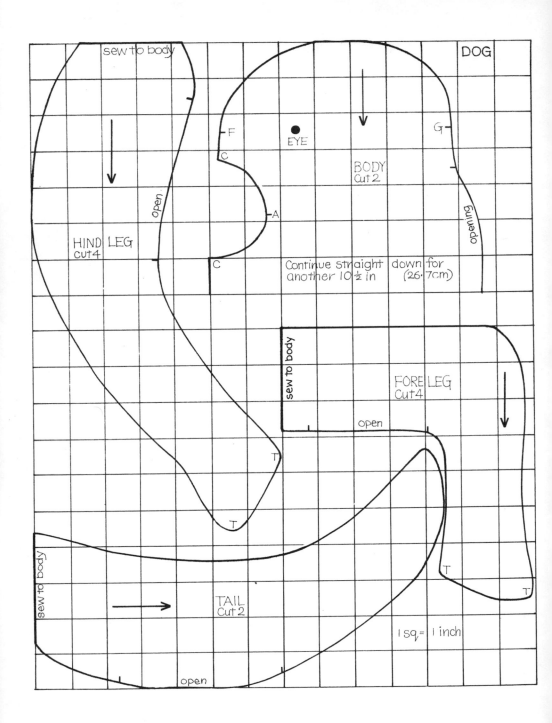

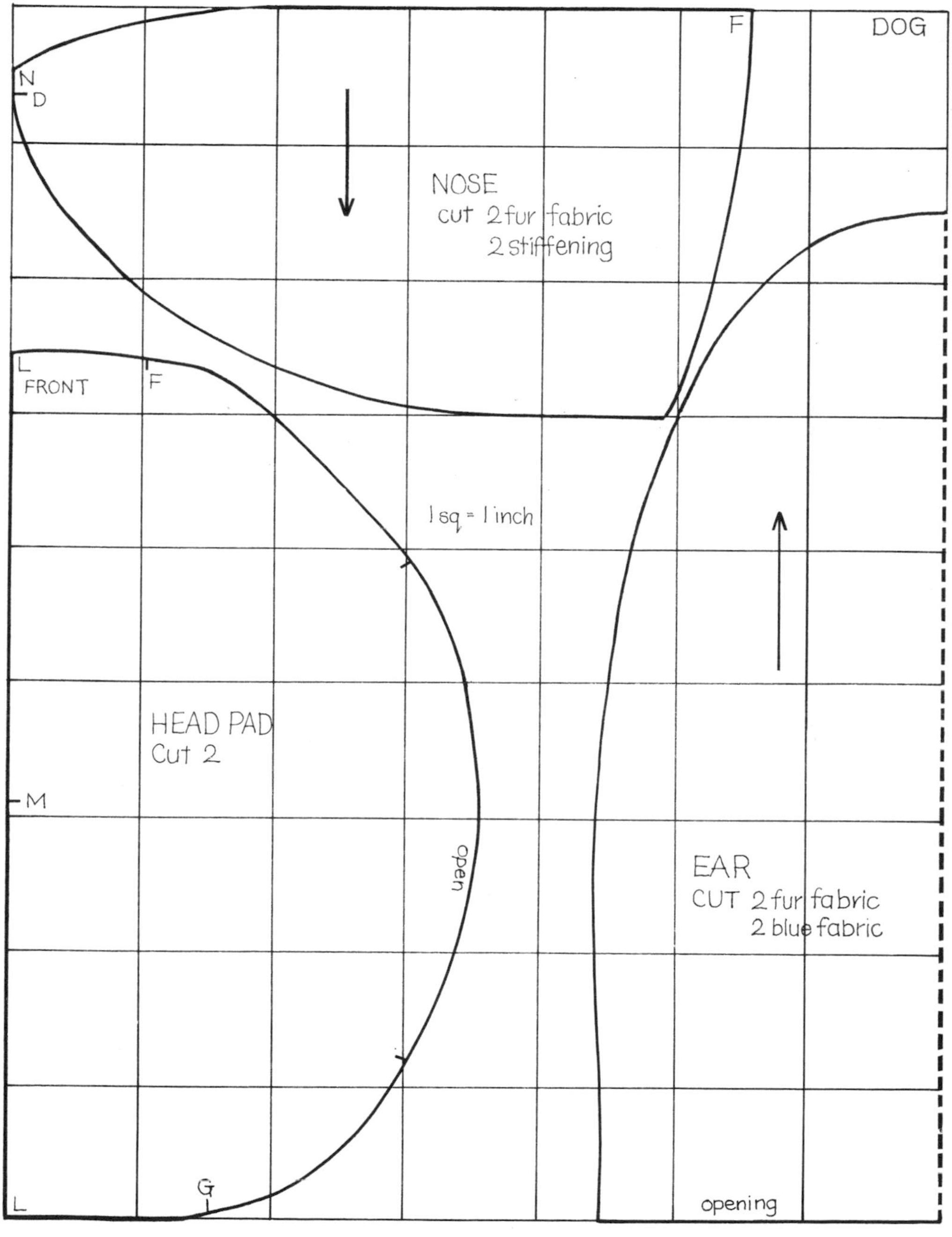

N
D

F   DOG

↓

NOSE
cut 2 fur fabric
    2 stiffening

L
FRONT   F

1 sq = 1 inch

↑

HEAD PAD
Cut 2

M

open

EAR
CUT 2 fur fabric
     2 blue fabric

L   G

opening

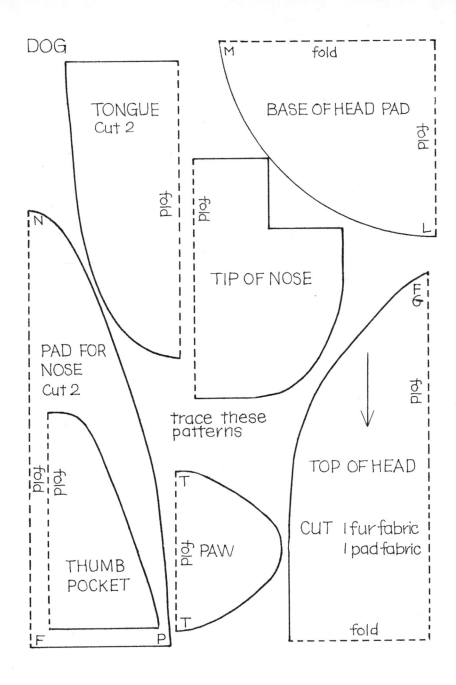

DOG

TONGUE
Cut 2

BASE OF HEAD PAD

M

L

fold

fold

TIP OF NOSE

fold

fold

N

PAD FOR
NOSE
Cut 2

F

G

trace these
patterns

fold

TOP OF HEAD

CUT 1 fur fabric
1 pad fabric

THUMB
POCKET

PAW

fold

fold

fold

T

T

F

P

fold

MATERIALS

1¼ yds (1 m 20 cm) blue fur fabric at 36 in (90 cm) wide or 1 yd (90 cm) of wider width; ¼ yd (30 cm) blue cotton and ¼ yd (30 cm) thin fabric any colour for pad both at 36 in (90 cm) wide; small pieces of red cotton and black satin; 9 in × 7 in (22·8 cm × 17·8 cm) interlining for stiffening; stiff card 5 in (12·7 cm) square; 2 joggle eyes; stuffing; thread in blue, red and black.

PATTERNS

Make paper patterns from squared diagrams as described at front of book. Thumb pocket is in paper only. Arrows on patterns show direction in which fur fabric should stroke.

Blue fur fabric Cut two bodies, two noses, four forelegs, four hindlegs and two tails, in all cases reversing patterns to make pairs, one top of head, one base of body, one lower mouth, and two ears. *Blue cotton* One inner mouth, one upper mouth, two ears and four paws. *Red cotton* Two tongues. *Black satin* One tip of nose. *Pad fabric* Two head pads, one top of head, one base of head pad, two pads for nose, two bases of body and one piece 16 in × 5 in (40·6 cm × 12·7 cm). *Stiffening* Two noses and one tongue stiffener. To get tongue stiffener pattern, cut tongue pattern then cut off ¼ in (6 mm) all round. *Card* Cut upper mouth pattern and cut off ¼ in (6 mm) all round.

SEWING

All backstitch is done ¼ in (6 mm) from edge.

MOUTH

Follow standard instructions, page 19.

Tongue Fig. 1 Tack stiffener to wrong side of one tongue. Pin two tongues together, wrong sides to outside. Backstitch round tongue, leaving straight edge open. Round opening turn edges to wrong side and tack down. Turn to right side. Oversew across opening. Remove tacking that held stiffening. Using red thread double sew straight edge of tongue to centre of mouth. Sew through inner mouth only, then check that finger and thumb pockets have not been closed.

Fig I

LEGS AND TAIL

Pin two forelegs, two hindlegs and two tails together, all wrong sides to outside. Using thread double backstitch, leaving openings where shown on patterns and between points T. Backstitch one blue cotton paw into end of each foreleg and hindleg matching points T. Round opening on forelegs, hindlegs and tail turn edge to wrong side and tack down. On foreleg snip surplus seam allowance at sharp bend. Turn all legs and tail to right side.

BODY

Mark position of eye from pattern. Sew one eye to right side of each body, using thread double. Sew one foreleg to right side of each body. Top point of foreleg, X on fig. 4, is $7\frac{1}{4}$ in (18·4 cm) down from top of body and halfway between the sides. Using thread double oversew edge of foreleg as shown dotted on fig. 4. Fold paw of foreleg onto body and tack it down temporarily to keep it well inside side seams.

Figs. 2 and 3 show top of head pattern and base of body pattern when opened out.

68

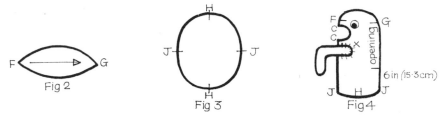

Fig 2

Fig 3

Fig 4

6in (15·3cm)

Fig. 4 Work on wrong sides and pin two bodies together. Pin top of head between bodies, matching points F and G. Using thread double backstitch from F to J at front of body, leaving opening between points C at mouth and from G to J at back of body, leaving opening in back for operator's hand. Backstitch right round top of head. At back opening turn edge ¼ in (6 mm) to wrong side and hem down. One turn is sufficient with fur fabric.

Using thread double backstitch base of body into end of body matching points H and J.

MOUTH INTO BODY

Turn to page 22 and follow standard instructions for Beak or Mouth into Body.

HEAD AND BODY PADS

Head pad Fig. 5 Use thread to mark front point on right side of one head as shown on pattern. Work on wrong sides and pin two head pads together. Backstitch from F to L and G to L. Pin in base of head pad matching points L and M and top of head pad matching points F and G. Backstitch right round base and one side of top, leaving opening as shown on second side of top.

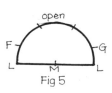

Fig 5

Fig 6

69

Base of body pad Fig. 6 Fold the long strip of pad fabric in half, wrong side to outside. Backstitch short sides together to form strip into a circle. Pin, then backstitch, a base of body into each end, keeping points J above each other. Leave an opening in one base.

Round openings in head and base of body pads turn edges to wrong side and tack down. Turn to right side. Stuff, keeping sides of pads well rounded but bases as flat as possible. Ladder stitch to close opening.

Pads into body Slip head pad through back of puppet into top of head. Back seam of head pad, GL, should match back seam of body. Peer up inside to check that front of head pad is lying on front seam of body. Make sure top of pad is fully into top of head. To sew pad in place use thread double and keep pressing pads upwards. Sew points L to seams of body where they touch. The front L should be just above centre top of mouth. Put hand into mouth and check that pad does not impede hand.

Slip base of body pad into foot of body. Working on inside of body sew the upper points J to front and back seams of body.

NOSE

Fig. 7 Tack a stiffener to wrong side of each nose. Pin two noses together, wrong sides to outside. Using thread double backstitch from D to F. Turn all other edges to wrong side and sew down. Small hemming stitches through turnover and stiffening will not show on right side. Turn to right side.

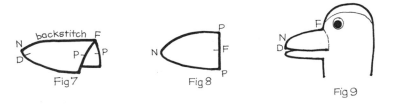

Fig. 8 Pin two nose pads together, wrong sides to outside. Backstitch round edge leaving PFP open. Round opening turn edge

70

to wrong side and tack down. Turn to right side. Stuff and ladder stitch to close opening.

Place pad inside nose, matching points F and N. Using blue thread double catch to tip of nose at N, sewing through seam surplus. Sew the two points P to the nose where they touch it, probably not at the outer edge, keeping pad pressed well up to top seam.

Fig. 9 Slip card support into upper mouth to give solidity for sewing. Pin nose to upper mouth, matching points D, then pin along edge of upper mouth. Using thread double ladder stitch these parts to upper mouth. Then pin point F of nose to F at end of top of head. Let rest of nose, shown dotted, lie naturally where it touches head. Using thread double ladder stitch from F to side of mouth. Remove card and check that hand still enters mouth.

Tip of nose Figs. 10 and 11 Working on wrong side bring points Q to meet and points R to meet. Backstitch QS and RS. Turn outside edge to wrong side and tack down. Turn to right side. Put in a little stuffing to round out tip of nose. Lay on end of dog's nose, matching points D. Using black thread ladder stitch round edge.

Fig 10   Fig 11

EARS

Pin one fur fabric ear and one cotton ear together, wrong side out. Backstitch edge, leaving straight edge open as shown on pattern. Round opening turn edge to wrong side and tack down. Turn to right side. Oversew across straight edge to close.

Fold ear in half, fur fabric to the outside. Using thread double ladder stitch top of each ear to head. Place it about one inch (2·5 cm) below the top of head seam and just behind eye. The fold of the ear is towards the back of the head. Sew across the top of the ear, lift the

71

ear up and sew back along the underside of the ear, then sew across
the top again.

FINISHING LEGS AND TAIL

Remove tacking to release forelegs. Stuff forelegs, hindlegs and tail,
only stuffing tail lightly. Using thread double ladder stitch to close
openings and to sew hindlegs and tail to body.

Forelegs Complete by sewing along underside to body, shown
dotted on fig. 12. Also sew between foreleg and body from upper to
lower edge of foreleg.

Hindlegs Top of leg is sewn along seam of body and base of body
about halfway between front and back seams. Sew right round top
of leg twice.

Toenails Sew toenails on each foreleg and hindleg, shown on fig.
12. Use black thread double and take straight stitches about $\frac{1}{2}$ in
(1·2 cm) long. Two stitches each side of centre seam. Sew over each
stitch about four times to make it prominent.

Tail Sew tail to end of body on centre back seam. Sew round
twice.

Finishing touch Check arm in puppet and see if it is possible to
close back opening a little by ladder stitching the sides together for
2 in (5·1 cm) at top of opening. This gives a better appearance but
people with stout arms, or who wear wide sleeves, may need the
whole opening.

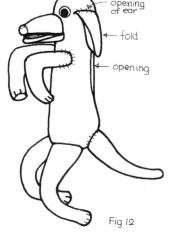

Fig 12

Didgeridoo the Kangaroo

Didgeridoo the Kangaroo is made in floral patterned fabric with a self-coloured front and carries two babies in her pouch, one of them stuffed and the other a finger puppet. The operator's hand enters at the centre back of the body. He can stand and hold the kangaroo upright or let her sit on his knee. Didgeridoo the Kangaroo is 21 in (53·3 cm) high and is 20 in (50·8 cm) from toe to tip of tail.

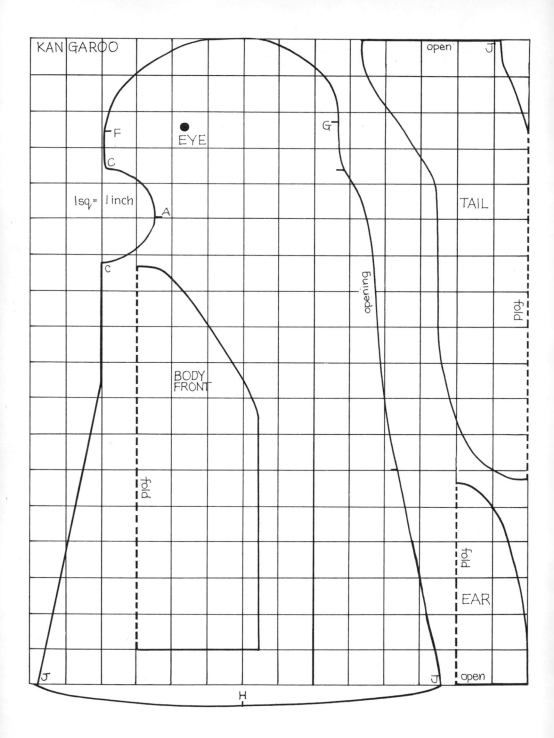

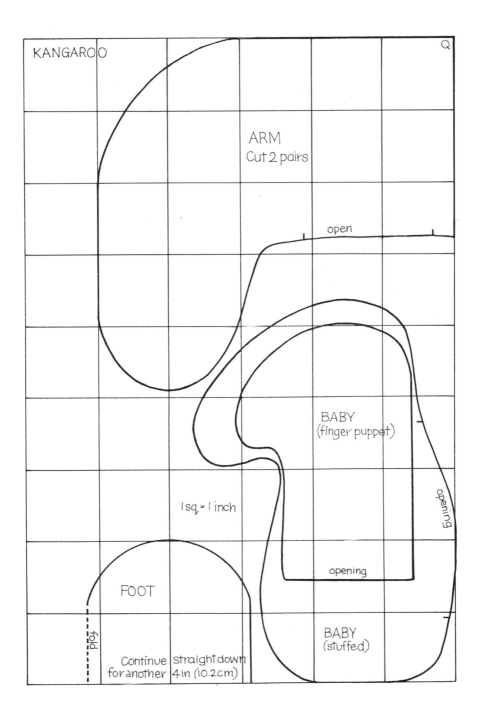

KANGAROO

ARM
Cut 2 pairs

open

BABY
(finger puppet)

opening

1 sq = 1 inch

opening

FOOT

fold

BABY
(stuffed)

Continue straight down
for another 4 in (10.2 cm)

Q

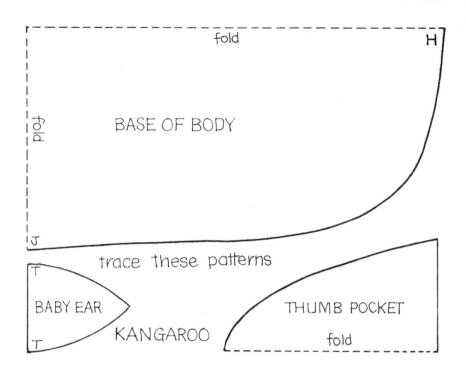

MATERIALS

1 yd (90 cm) mauve patterned floral fabric, $\frac{1}{3}$ yd (30 cm) mauve fabric, $\frac{1}{2}$ yd (40 cm) thin fabric any colour for pads, all at 36 in (90 cm) wide; 8 in × 5 in (20·3 cm × 12·7 cm) orange fabric; 12 in × 3 in (30·5 cm × 7·6 cm) interlining for stiffening; stiff card 5 in (12·7 cm) square; two joggle eyes; stuffing and thread in mauve, white and black.

PATTERNS

Make paper patterns from squared diagrams as described at front of book. Copy inner mouth, upper and lower mouth from dog (page

76

63). Copy nose, head pad, base of head pad, top of head and pad for nose from Dog (pages 65 and 66). Thumb pocket is in paper only.

Floral fabric Cut two bodies, two noses, four arms and two babies of each type, in all cases reversing patterns to make pairs, one top of head, one base of body, one upper mouth, one lower mouth, four ears and one tail. *Mauve fabric* One body front, two feet and one pouch measuring 7 in × 4 in (17·8 cm × 10·2 cm). *Orange fabric* One inner mouth. *Pad fabric* Two head pads, one top of head, one base of head pad, two pads for nose, two bases of body and one piece 24 in × 5 in (61 cm × 12·7 cm). *Stiffening* Two noses and two baby's ears. *Card* Cut upper mouth pattern and cut off $\frac{1}{4}$ in (6 mm) all round.

SEWING

All backstitch is done $\frac{1}{4}$ in (6 mm) from edge.

MOUTH

Follow standard instructions, page 19. Sew thumb pocket in mauve thread.

MOUTH INTO BODY

Mark position of eye from pattern. Sew one eye to right side of each body, using thread double.

Work on wrong side and pin two bodies together. Using thread double backstitch from F to J at front of body, leaving opening between points C at mouth. Now turn to page 22 and follow standard instructions for Beak or Mouth into Body.

BODY

Pouch Turn top edge over twice to wrong side and hem or machine. Turn other three sides $\frac{1}{4}$ in (6 mm) to wrong side and tack down. Press.

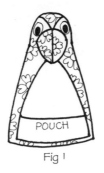

Fig 1

Front Fig. 1 Turn all edges of front of body $\frac{1}{4}$ in (6 mm) to wrong side and tack down. Press. On body of kangaroo open out seam from C to H and press it flat. Working on right side of body pin on the front, putting it in the centre and about $\frac{1}{2}$ in (1·2 cm) above the bottom edge. Using mauve thread double, hem round all edges of front of body using as small stitches as possible.

Pin the pouch on top of the front. The hem is at the top. Using thread double hem along each side and across the bottom. Stitch very firmly at top corners and sew for about $\frac{1}{2}$ in (1·2 cm) from top corners along top of pouch.

Figs. 2 and 3 Show top of head pattern and base of body pattern when opened out.

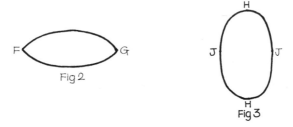

Fig 2

Fig 3

Work on wrong sides and pin two bodies together. Pin top of head between bodies matching points F and G. Using thread double, backstitch from G to J at back of body, leaving opening in back for puppeteer's hand, also backstitch right round top of head. At back opening turn edge over twice to wrong side and hem down.

78

Using thread double, backstitch base of body into end of body matching points H and J. Turn to right side.

Fig 4

HEAD AND BODY PADS AND NOSE

Turn to page 69 and follow instructions for Dog. Kangaroo has not been given tip of nose but you could add it if you wish.

EARS

Pin two ears together, wrong sides out. Backstitch edges, leaving base open as shown on pattern. Round opening turn edge to wrong side and tack down. Turn to right side. Oversew across base to close.

Fold each corner to centre. Using thread double oversew across base.

Fig. 4 Using thread double ladder stitch base of each ear to head. Ear is upright with folded corners facing front. Base lies half on top of head, half on body. Sew round twice.

LIMBS AND TAIL

Pin arms together in pairs, fold each foot and fold tail, all wrong sides to outside. Using thread double, backstitch leaving openings where shown on pattern. Round openings turn edge to wrong side and tack down. On arm snip surplus seam allowance at sharp bend. Turn all pieces to right side. Stuff. Using thread double ladder stitch to close opening on arms and feet. Leave tail open. Use ladder stitch, with thread double, to sew all limbs and tail to body.

79

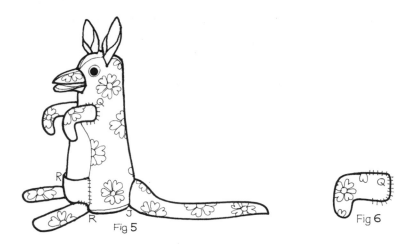

Fig 5

Fig 6

Arms Figs. 5 and 6 Point Q is level with top of mauve front and straight down from ear. Fig. 6 Sew straight end first, sewing along twice, then sew each side about halfway to elbow joint. Keep tilting arm slightly upwards while sewing.

Fig 7

Feet Fig. 7 The end RS is sewn to front of body just below mauve front. RS is parallel with ground. Place so that folded side, ending at R, comes to the outside of each foot. Ladder stitch twice round RS. On second round, while crossing front of foot, hold foot tilted up slightly and take stitches well up front of body so that foot does not sag down.

Tail Fig. 5 Open end of tail will be circular. Place point J to point J at back seam of body. Ladder stitch twice round end of tail.

STUFFED BABY

Fig 8 Pin two babies together, wrong sides to outside. Using thread double backstitch right round, leaving opening as shown. Round

80

Fig 8

opening turn edges to wrong side and tack down. Turn to right side and stuff. Ladder stitch to close opening. Use black thread double for eyes, nose and mouth. Sew over nose and mouth three times to give a solid line.

Fold bottom corner of each ear to centre. Catch down with white thread and sew ear to side of head.

FINGER PUPPET BABY

Use black thread double to sew an eye to right side of each baby. Make ears as in 'stuffed baby' and sew one to each side of head. Pin two babies together, wrong sides to outside and tuck in ears to avoid them being caught in seam. Using thread double backstitch round sides, leaving straight end open. Round opening turn edges to wrong side and sew down. Snip seam allowance under chin. Turn to right side. Use black thread to sew nose and mouth.

PLAYING WITH BABY

Didgeridoo can bend forward, catch baby's head in her mouth and pull it out of pouch. To return baby to pouch Didgeridoo's mouth can hold baby's head and guide him in but puppeteer's other hand has to hold open the pouch and give a little help.

Big Bad Bertie Rabbit

Bad Bertie is a really large puppet, designed for sitting on the operator's knee. He also looks very impressive held upright when operator is standing. Made in brown fur fabric he looks luxurious and measures 46 in (117 cm) high.

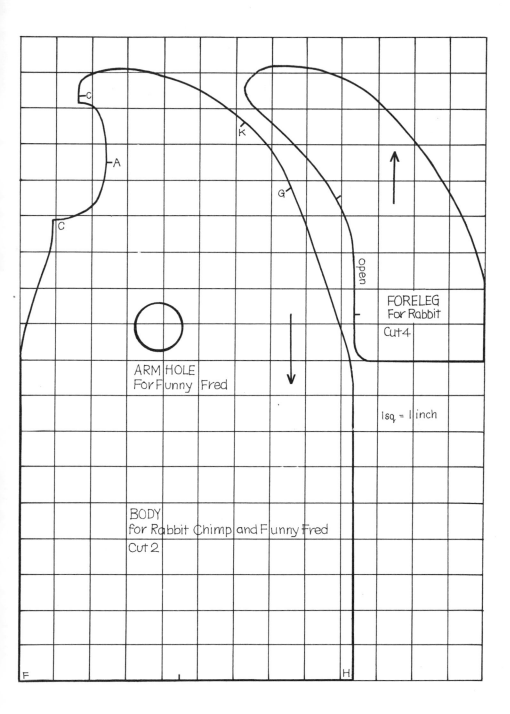

C

A

C

K

G

open

FORELEG
For Rabbit

Cut 4

ARM HOLE
For Funny Fred

1 sq = 1 inch

BODY
for Rabbit Chimp and Funny Fred

Cut 2

F

H

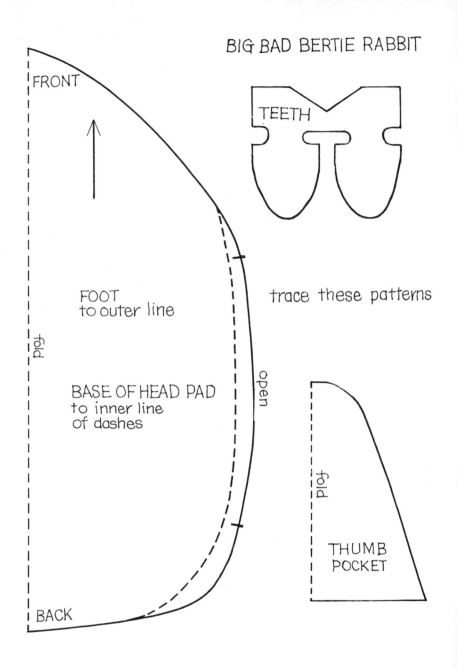

BIG BAD BERTIE RABBIT

TEETH

FRONT

FOOT
to outer line

fold

BASE OF HEAD PAD
to inner line
of dashes

open

BACK

trace these patterns

fold

THUMB
POCKET

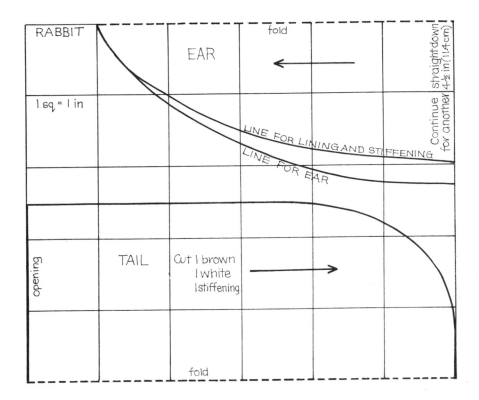

MATERIALS

1½ yds (1 m 30 cm) brown fur fabric at 36 in (90 cm) wide or 1 yd (90 cm) if wider; 10 in × 8 in (25·4 cm × 20·3 cm) red fabric; 20 in × 10 in (50·8 cm × 25·4 cm) yellow fabric; 7 in × 6 in (17·8 cm × 15·3 cm) white fur fabric; ⅓ yd (30 cm) at 36 in (90 cm) wide of thin fabric any colour for pads; 15 in × 10 in (38·1 cm × 25·4 cm) interlining for stiffening; 4 in (10·2 cm) square stiff card; 2 in (5·1 cm) square white plastic from detergent container; two joggle eyes; stuffing and brown thread.

PATTERNS

Make paper patterns from squared diagrams as described at front of book. Copy inner mouth, upper and lower mouth from Dog (page 63). Copy head from Snail (page 55) but reletter it as shown in fig. 1. Thumb pocket is in paper only.

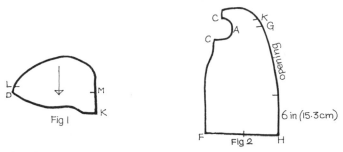

Fig 1

Fig 2

6 in (15·3cm)

Brown fur fabric Cut two bodies, two heads and four forelegs in all cases reversing patterns to make pairs, one lower mouth, pile stroking from E to C, four feet, two ears cut to outer line on pattern, one tail, one circle 5½ in (14 cm) in diameter and two pieces each 20 in × 6 in (50·8 cm × 15·3 cm) for legs. *Red fabric* One inner mouth and one upper mouth. *Yellow fabric* Two ear linings cut to inner line on pattern. *White fur fabric* One tail. *Pad fabric* Two head pads, one base of head pad, two circles each 5½ in (14 cm) in diameter and one piece 18 in × 6 in (45·7 cm × 15·3 cm). *Stiffening* Two ear stiffeners cut to inner line on pattern and one tail. *Card* Cut upper mouth pattern and cut off ¼ in (6 mm) all round. *White plastic* One set of teeth.

SEWING

All backstitch is done ¼ in (6 mm) from edge.

MOUTH

Follow standard instructions, page 19. Sew thumb pocket in brown thread.

86

BODY

Fig. 2 Mark point K on right side of one body with thread, about $\frac{1}{2}$ in (1·2 cm) from edge. Pin two bodies together, wrong sides to outside. Using thread double backstitch from C above mouth right round top of body to H, leaving opening in back for puppeteer's hand. Backstitch from C below mouth to F.

Pin fur fabric circle into foot of body as base. Backstitch in place using thread double. At back opening turn edge $\frac{1}{4}$ in (6 mm) to wrong side and hem down. One turn is sufficient with fur fabric.

MOUTH INTO BODY

Turn to page 22 and follow standard instructions for Beak or Mouth into Body.

SEWING REMAINING PARTS

Using thread double sew an eye to right side of each head. Pattern shows position.

Heads Figs. 3 and 4 Pin two heads together and two head pads together, all wrong sides to outside. Backstitch heads from D over the top to K and head pad over the top, using thread double on head. Round open end of head, turn edge $\frac{1}{4}$ in (6 mm) to wrong side and tack down. Turn head to right side. Pin base of head pad into open end of head pad, matching front and back points. Backstitch round edge, leaving opening for stuffing in one side.

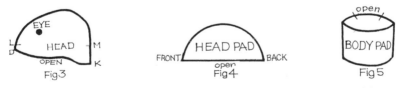

Fig.3 Fig.4 Fig.5

Body pad Fig. 5 Fold the long strip of pad fabric in half, wrong side to outside. Backstitch short sides together to form strip into a circle. Pin, then backstitch, a pad fabric circle into each end. Leave an opening in one circle.

Forelegs, feet and tail Tack stiffening to wrong side of one tail. Pin two forelegs, two feet and two tails together, all wrong sides to outside. Using brown thread double, backstitch, leaving openings where shown on patterns.

Hindleg Fold each straight strip for leg in half, wrong side to outside. Using thread double backstitch the long side, leaving a gap of about $4\frac{1}{2}$ in (11·4 cm) near one end. Gather round each short end, using thread double. Pull up tight and finish off thread.

Ears Tack an ear stiffener to wrong side of a yellow lining. Tack yellow lining to brown fur ear wrong sides to outside. Fur ear is wider than lining and stiffener. Pin carefully down one long side, keeping edges together. Pin the other long side. The fur will curve more at the back which gives a realistic effect to finished ear. Backstitch each long side.

At openings left in head pad, body pad, forelegs, feet, tail, hindlegs and ears turn edges of opening to wrong side and tack down. Turn to right side. Stuff head pad and body pad keeping bases flat. Stuff forelegs. Stuff feet very lightly. Stuff hindlegs lightly. Ladder stitch to close openings on all these parts and on ears.

FINISHING BODY

Hold head upside down and slip head pad into it, front to point L, back to point M. Make sure that curved top of pad fits properly into curved top of head. When satisfied with fit use brown thread double and sew pad to inside of head at L and M. Stitch on the seam allowance of the head and stitches will not show on outside.

Fig. 6 Trim the sides of the card until it fits neatly into upper mouth. It lets one pin and sew without fear of closing mouth and gives some solidity for the sewing. Pin the head to the top of the body. Match points K first at back of head and body. Then pin point D. Head looks best if sitting straight up from point D and not sagging back. Fingers in finger pocket need room so make sure that head pad is not pressing down on mouth. Pin sides of head along edge of upper mouth from D then straight across body to K. Using thread double ladder stitch round head, leaving about 3 in (7·6 cm) unsewn at point D. Remove card.

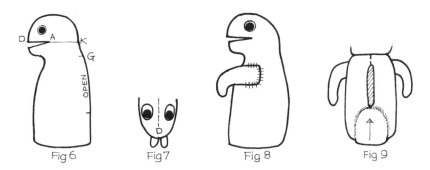

Fig 6   Fig 7   Fig 8   Fig 9

Teeth Fig. 7 Slip teeth into front of mouth at point D, so that just the two teeth protrude. The narrow necks of the teeth come at seam line. Finish ladder stitching the head to the body sewing round the neck of the teeth as they are reached. A few oversewing stitches are easiest between the two teeth. It is not necessary to sew through the plastic as the straight top of the teeth which is inside the mouth ensures that they cannot fall out.

Body pad Slip pad into foot of body. Working on inside of body use brown thread to sew the top to front and back seams of body.

Forelegs Fig. 8 Sew one foreleg to each side of body, using ladder stitch, with thread double. Sew straight end first, sewing front and back of this end with large stitches to hold it in place. Do not finish off thread. Sew on second foreleg similarly. Check whether forelegs are placed evenly. If correct finish thread. Take a new double thread. Sew round this short end again taking smaller, more secure, stitches, then sew along lower side of foreleg for about one inch (2·5 cm), up underside between foreleg and body, then back along top side to reach straight end again. Fasten off.

Tail Fig. 9 Sew tail to centre back of body, white fur side to outside. Using brown thread double ladder stitch twice along base of tail. Catch centre top of tail to body with a few stitches taken on brown side of tail.

Hindlegs Ladder stitch hindlegs to base of body, using thread double. Seam of hindleg faces back of body. Start and finish on outsides of each hindleg and sew round twice.

Bend each hindleg at knee so that a crease forms across back of knee. Using thread double ladder stitch along this crease from one side of knee along back of knee to other side. This holds knee in bent position. Leg looks good when rabbit is held at arm's length and also lets it sit easily on knee. Hindleg can be left straight if preferred.

Foot Sew a foot to end of each hindleg. Back of foot goes at centre back of hindleg. Using thread double ladder stitch round leg twice. Sewing is easiest if puppet is held upside down.

Ears Fold bottom corners to centre front on top of lining. Catch down with a few stitches.

Fig. 10 Sew an ear to each side of head, ladder stitching twice round base, using thread double. Yellow lining faces outwards at side of head. Second time round sew higher up on brown fur side to hold ear in upright position.

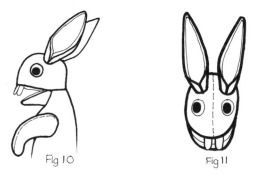

Fig. 11 Ears placed to face front of head, and sticking out sideways, are actually wrong but many people like them this way.

90

Chippy the Chimp

Chippy the Chimp is another really large puppet designed for sitting on the puppeteer's knee. He also looks very impressive held upright when puppeteer is standing as he is 40 in (101·56 cm) high. He is made in brown fur fabric with a cheerful yellow fur fabric face and fawn cloth ears, feet and hands. As the mouth is stiffened, with pads above and below it, it opens and shuts but cannot be twisted sideways.

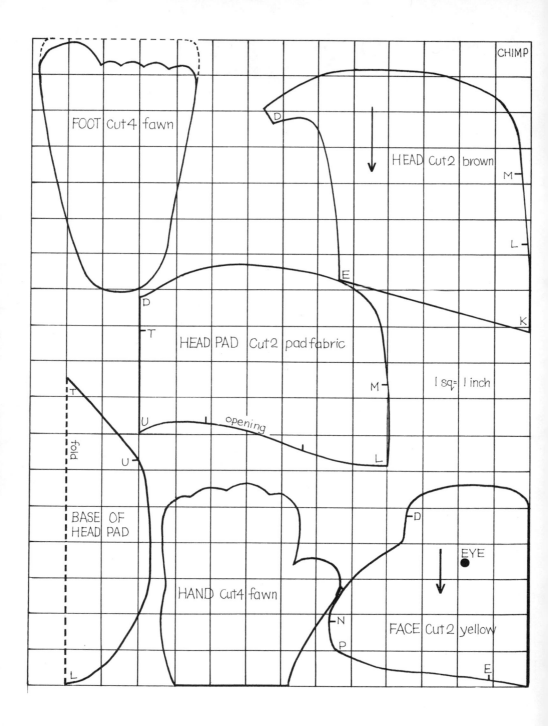

FOOT Cut 4 fawn

CHIMP

HEAD Cut 2 brown

D

M

L

K

D

T

HEAD PAD Cut 2 pad fabric

E

M

1 sq = 1 inch

T

fold

U

opening

L

U

BASE OF
HEAD PAD

HAND Cut 4 fawn

D

EYE

N

P

FACE Cut 2 yellow

E

L

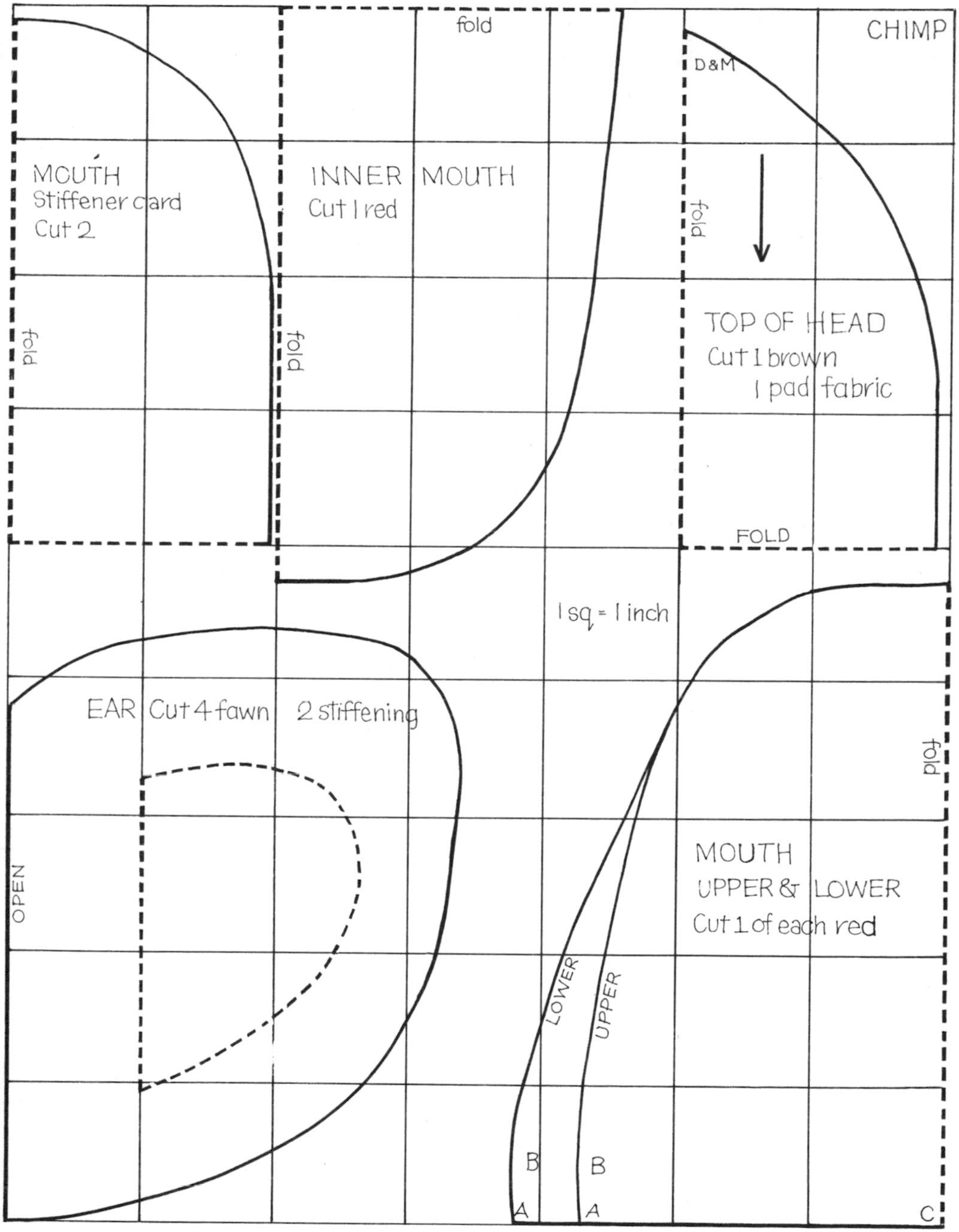

CHIMP

MOUTH
Stiffener card
Cut 2

INNER MOUTH
Cut 1 red

D&M

fold

fold

fold

fold

TOP OF HEAD
Cut 1 brown
1 pad fabric

FOLD

1 sq = 1 inch

EAR Cut 4 fawn   2 stiffening

OPEN

fold

MOUTH
UPPER & LOWER
Cut 1 of each red

LOWER

UPPER

B

B

A

A

C

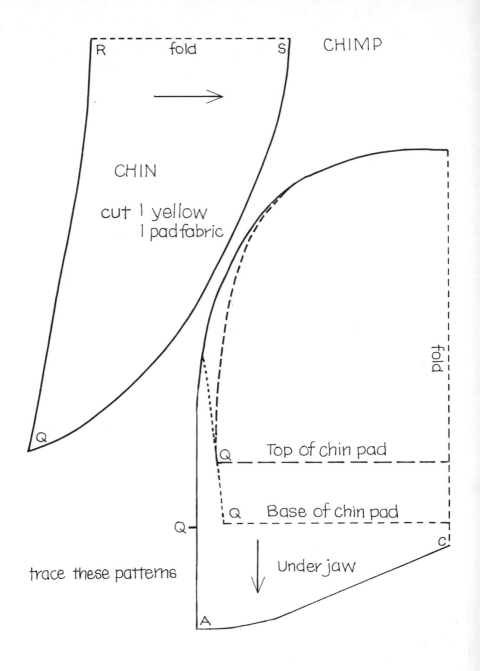

R   fold   S   CHIMP

CHIN

cut 1 yellow
    1 pad fabric

Q

Q   Top of chin pad

Q   Base of chin pad

Q

fold

c

trace these patterns

Under jaw

A

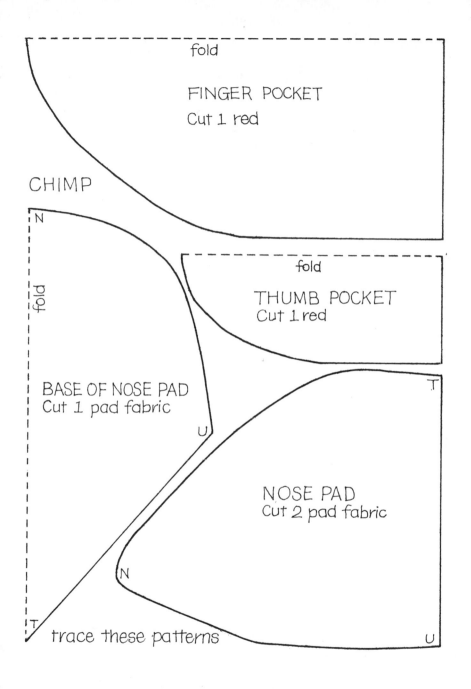

fold

FINGER POCKET
Cut 1 red

CHIMP

N

fold

fold

THUMB POCKET
Cut 1 red

BASE OF NOSE PAD
Cut 1 pad fabric

T

U

NOSE PAD
Cut 2 pad fabric

N

T

trace these patterns

U

MATERIALS

$1\frac{1}{8}$ yds (1 m) brown fur fabric at 36 in (90 cm) wide or 1 yd (90 cm) if wider; 6 in (15·3 cm) yellow fur fabric, $\frac{1}{2}$ yd (40 cm) fawn fabric such as brushed courtelle, $\frac{1}{3}$ yd (30 cm) red fabric and $\frac{1}{2}$ yd (50 cm) thin fabric any colour for pads, all at 36 in (90 cm) wide; 8 in × 5 in (20·3 cm × 12·7 cm) interlining for stiffening; two pieces each 4 in (10·2 cm) square stiff card or plastic from detergent container for stiffening mouth; 20 in (50·8 cm) thin rope and $20\frac{1}{2}$ in (52 cm) wire for tail; two joggle eyes; stuffing and thread in brown, yellow, fawn and red.

PATTERNS

Make paper patterns from squared diagrams as described at front of book. Body pattern is on page 83.

Brown fur fabric Cut out two bodies and two heads, reversing pattern to make pairs, one top of head, one under-jaw cut full size of pattern, one circle $5\frac{1}{2}$ in (14 cm) in diameter, two pieces each 20 in × 5 in (50·8 cm × 12·7 cm) for arms, two pieces each 20 in × 6 in (50·8 cm × 15·3 cm) for legs and one piece 21 in × 2 in (53·3 cm × 5·1 cm) for tail. On arms, legs and tail pile strokes along the length. *Yellow fur fabric* Two faces and one chin. *Fawn fabric* Four ears cut to full size of pattern and four hands reversing pattern to make pairs. Cut two feet with toes as shown on pattern. Cut two more feet cut roughly to dotted line on pattern without shaped toes. One foot with toes and one roughly cut foot to go together to make a pair. *Red fabric* One inner mouth, one upper mouth, one lower mouth, one finger pocket and one thumb pocket. Four mouth stiffener covers which are obtained by cutting paper pattern for 'mouth stiffener card' and cutting the fabric $\frac{1}{4}$ in (6 mm) larger all round. *Pad fabric* Two head pads, one top of head, one base of head pad, two nose pads, one base of nose pad, one chin, one top of chin pad cut to pattern line of dashes, one base of chin pad cut to pattern line of dots, two circles each $5\frac{1}{2}$ in (14 cm) in diameter and one piece 18 in

96

× 6 in (45·7 cm × 15·3 cm). *Stiffening* Two ears cut to full size of pattern. *Card or plastic* Two mouth stiffeners as pattern. *Paper* Cut two ears to inner dotted line on pattern.

SEWING

All backstitch is done $\frac{1}{4}$ in (6 mm) from edge.

MOUTH

Follow standard instructions, page 19, without sewing thumb pocket. The lower and upper mouths are wider than the inner mouth. Put the outer edges together and let the fullness stay in the middle. Overcast along each edge AA to prevent fraying.

Turn straight edge of four mouth stiffener covers, of finger pocket and of thumb pocket $\frac{1}{4}$ in (6 mm) to wrong side. Sew down with running stitch which will stay in place.

Fig. 1 Pin finger pocket to one mouth stiffener cover wrong sides to outside.

Fig. 2 Mark centre of another mouth stiffener cover. Pin thumb pocket to it, wrong sides to outside, so that each edge of thumb pocket is $\frac{3}{4}$ in (2 cm) from centre point of mouth stiffener cover. Thumb pocket stands up in a curve. Pin rest of thumb pocket keeping in line with these points so that whole of thumb pocket is curved and spacious. Using thread double backstitch round curved edge of finger and of thumb pockets, leave straight edge open. Test pockets for size.

Fig 1

Fig 2

Fig 3

Fig. 3 Keep each section with finger or thumb pocket uppermost. Pin another mouth stiffener cover behind each section. The new

97

covers have their wrong sides touching the existing sections and right sides facing outwards. Backstitch round the outer curve of the mouth stiffener covers. Slip a mouth stiffener card or plastic into each section between the mouth stiffener covers. Oversew the straight edges of the covers to hold card in place but be careful not to sew through the finger or thumb pockets.

Fig. 4 Slip these mouth stiffeners through the gap at AA into the upper and lower mouths, so that the card sides lie next to the inner mouth. The finger pocket is in the upper mouth and the thumb pocket in the lower mouth. Sew the edge of the finger pocket to upper mouth along line BB. A hemming stitch is easiest.

UPPER MOUTH   LOWER MOUTH
Fig 4

Stiffened cover
Fig 5

Fig. 5 The thumb pocket is similarly sewn to the lower mouth, but it is important to keep the surplus fabric curved for the thumb. Press the corners of the stiffener well into the lower mouth. Start sewing stiffener to lower mouth, line BB, at each outer edge as shown by arrows on fig. 5. Let the surplus fabric of lower mouth fall loosely round the thumb pocket. Then sew thumb pocket and rest of lower mouth to each other.

Checking When puppet is in use puppeteer's hand has to guide itself into finger and thumb pockets by feel. Fold the mouth for speaking and gaps appear between stiffeners and inner mouth where fingers could stray. Using red thread double ladder stitch across to close these gaps, just catching inside of each stiffener to inner mouth where they touch, probably about $\frac{1}{4}$ in (6 mm) down the inside. Keep forefinger of non-sewing hand in bend of folded

98

mouth so that the needle only picks up fabric from inner mouth. Do not sew the two stiffeners together. This looks obvious but pulls the thumb pocket and makes it feel tight.

BODY

Turn to page 87 and follow instructions for Rabbit. Pin fur fabric circle into foot of body as base. It helps to place base evenly if it is lightly folded in half, then in half again and points marked at these quarters as shown. These points can be matched to points on body. Backstitch in place using thread double. At back opening of body turn edge $\frac{1}{4}$ in (6 mm) to wrong side and hem down. One turn is sufficient with fur fabric.

MOUTH INTO BODY

Fig. 6 Mark centre of upper and lower mouths which are points C. Body is wrong side out, mouth right side out. Hold mouth and slip it through the mouth hole in body like posting a letter. Slip the tip of the mouth in first and finger pocket should be on top. Push it through till mouth is on right side of body and line AA matches points AA on body. Mouth is shown dotted between the two bodies.

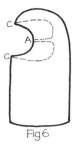

Fig 6

Still working on wrong side of body pin mouth and body together. To keep fullness round thumb pocket start pinning at centre top of mouth, matching points C on finger pocket and body. Pin round sides. Pin along lower mouth from each side letting fullness gather round thumb pocket. Now pin thumb pocket to body matching points C. Using brown thread double backstitch about $\frac{1}{2}$ in (1·2 cm) from edge. Aim at this measurement but it may be less at points A where it is a little tricky to sew.

Slit the seam allowance at A on each side. Turn body to right side. Put hand into mouth and check that all is well.

HEAD AND FACE

Fig. 7 On each head make three small slits in corner of curve. Turn edge DE $\frac{1}{4}$ in (6 mm) to wrong side and tack down. The dots on the figure show where it turns.

Fig. 8 Mark position of eye on each yellow face as shown on pattern. Also mark point N on one face. Working with right side uppermost lay brown head on top of yellow face, matching points D and E. Using brown thread double sew along DE. Small hemming stitches will not be seen in pile of fur. Repeat with other face and head. Using yellow thread double sew an eye to each face.

Pin the two heads together, wrong sides to outside. Pin a brown fur top of head between points D and M with pile stroking from D to M. Using yellow thread double backstitch from P to D. Using brown thread double backstitch right round top of head and from M to K. Turn edge PK $\frac{1}{4}$ in (6 mm) to wrong side and tack down. Turn to right side.

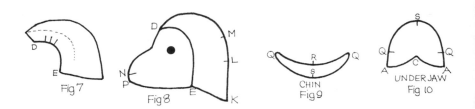

Figs. 9 and 10 Using brown thread double backstitch yellow fur chin and brown fur under-jaw together, wrong sides to outside, matching points Q and S. Turn edge QRQ of chin and QACAQ of

100

under-jaw $\frac{1}{4}$ in (6 mm) to wrong side and tack down. Turn to right side.

STUFFED PADS

Nose and head pads have strange shapes when stuffed. To identify which way to handle them mark, on right side of fabric about $\frac{1}{2}$ in (1·2 cm) from edge, point N on nose pad and point D on head pad.

All pads are sewn with wrong sides to outside using backstitch $\frac{1}{4}$ in (6 mm) from edge. Round openings turn edge $\frac{1}{4}$ in (6 mm) to wrong side and tack down. Stuff and ladder stitch to close opening.

Nose pad Sew two nose pads together from N to T. Sew base of nose pad between them matching points TUN, leaving an opening in one side between N and U. When stuffing keep line NT well rounded. Stuff firmly but try not to let NU sag down.

Head pad Sew two head pads together from D to T and from M to L. Sew top of head between them matching points D and M. Sew base of head pad between them matching points TUL, leaving an opening in one side between U and L as shown on pattern. Stuff not too firmly but try to keep shape well rounded over top of head.

Fig. 11 Join nose and head pads together at the flat sides. Using thread double ladder stitch twice right round TU.

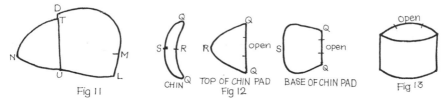

Fig 11   CHIN TOP OF CHIN PAD   BASE OF CHIN PAD   Fig 13
Fig 12

Chin pad Fig. 12 Sew top of chin pad to chin which is cut in pad fabric matching points QRQ. Sew base of chin pad to chin matching points QSQ. Join top and base together for about one inch (2·5 cm) from Q leaving rest as opening. When stuffing keep chin well rounded at R and S, but taper off the stuffing towards Q.

Body pad Fig. 13 Fold the long strip of pad fabric in half and sew

101

the short sides together to form a circle. Pin, then sew, a pad fabric circle into each. Leave an opening in one circle. When stuffing keep circles as flat as possible.

ARMS AND LEGS

Fold each arm or leg piece in half lengthwise. Tack, then using thread double backstitch the long side. About $3\frac{1}{2}$ in (8·9 cm) from top end leave an opening of about $4\frac{1}{2}$ in (11·4 cm). Pile of fur should stroke down from top. Round opening turn edge $\frac{1}{4}$ in (6 mm) to wrong side and tack down. Using thread double gather each short end. Pull up and finish off thread. Turn to right side. Stuff and ladder stitch to close opening.

FEET, HANDS AND EARS

Figs. 14 and 15 Pin ears, feet and hands together, in pairs, wrong sides to outside. One roughly cut foot and one correctly cut foot go together. On feet and hands it is helpful to mark a sewing line $\frac{1}{4}$ in (6 mm) from edge of toes or fingers. Ball pen used lightly will do. Without a guide line it is easy to lose the curved effect when sewing. This line is shown dotted on figs. 14 and 15. Pin an interlining ear on top of each pair of ears. Using thread double backstitch all round each foot, hand or ear leaving openings as shown. Round openings turn edge $\frac{1}{4}$ in (6 mm) to wrong side and tack down. Cut away surplus fabric from roughly cut foot. Snip down between toes and fingers to sewing line on each foot and hand to help it to turn out smoothly. Turn all pieces to right side.

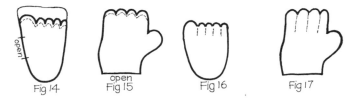

Fig 14   Fig 15   Fig 16   Fig 17

Feet Fig. 16 Stuff feet, keeping stuffing thin at toes. Ladder stitch to close opening. Use fawn thread and stab-stitch between

102

each toe for one inch (2·5 cm) sewing through both sides and pulling thread tight, as shown by dotted lines.

Hands Fig. 17 Stuff finger end of hand lightly. Use fawn thread and stab-stitch between fingers as shown by dotted lines. Sew through both sides, pulling thread tight. Stuff thumb and rest of hand, leaving wrist open. Gather round edge of wrist. Pull up and finish off thread.

Ears Sew across opening to close it. Pin one of the paper ears on to each ear. Use fawn thread and stab-stitch just outside edge of paper, sewing through both thicknesses of fabric. Remove paper. This sewn line on ear improves its appearance.

TAIL

Use pliers to turn over each end of wire to lose sharp point. Lay wire along rope. Hold wire and rope together by winding thread round it along the full length. On brown fur tail turn over one long side and both short ends $\frac{1}{4}$ in (6 mm) to wrong side and tack down.

Working on wrong side lay wired rope close to the long side that has not been turned over. Roll up until other long end is reached.

Using thread double hem along length. Stitch across each short end to close it. Rope tries to twist making it tricky to hold tail in position for sewing. As fabric is rolled up stick some pins through rope and fabric but only put them half in so that a conspicuous bit of pin shows. This controls tail sufficiently to sew it without risk of leaving a pin in the fur. While sewing take an occasional stitch right through the rope.

ASSEMBLY

Head pad into head Put nose/head pad into the fur fabric head, pushing it in well as it is to round out the head. Using thread double sew point N of nose pad to N on face and L of head pad to L on back of head. In both cases sew through the seam allowance on the inside.

Head to body Fig. 18 Pin the head to the top of the body. Match points K first at back of head and body. Then pin point P to tip of upper mouth. Pin sides of head along edge of upper mouth from P then across body to K. Using thread double, ladder stitch round head. Sew head first starting at K with brown thread, then use yellow thread round face.

Completing chin Fig. 19 Slip chin pad into the yellow fur chin and brown fur under-jaw. In sketch chin pad is blank, yellow fur chin is dotted and brown fur under-jaw is shaded. Top of chin pad is uppermost. Catch point R of chin pad to R of fur chin with a few stitches in yellow thread. Hold the pad and pull the brown fur fabric taut. This helps to round the bottom of the chin. Catch chin pad along line QQ. Use brown thread with small stitches through fur but large stitches can be on pad as they will not show.

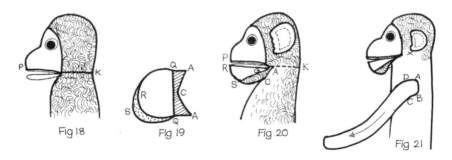

Fig 18   Fig 19   Fig 20   Fig 21

Chin to body Fig. 20 Pin chin/under-jaw to body, pinning AQR round lower mouth. Point C goes as near to point C on body as you can. It is tempting to put C about opposite S but this gives the chimp a double chin. Pull point C right up to just under the mouth and give the face a good jawline when viewed sideways. Using thread double, ladder stitch all round, yellow thread along QRQ, brown thread along tiny section QA, then round underneath jaw at ACA.

Ear to head Fig. 20 Using fawn thread double, ladder stitch twice round straight side of ear.

Put hand into puppet and check that finger and thumb pockets are still open.

Arms to body Fig. 21 Take time to do this as it is tricky sewing a

104

stuffed arm to an empty body. Lay chimp on table for support. Arrow shows way pile of fur fabric should stroke. Point A of arm is about 5 in (12·7 cm) down from base of ear and about 2 in (5·1 cm) further back. Seam of arm is best on underside or halfway up inside. Using thread double ladder stitch twice round end at AB. Take new double thread. Ladder stitch along from B for 2 in (5·2 cm) to C, between body and arm from C to D then along to A. Sew round a second time. When sewing second arm stop at each stage before finishing off thread and check that arms are evenly placed.

Body pad into body Slip pad into foot of body. Working on inside of body use brown thread to sew the top to front and back seams of body.

Legs to body Ladder stitch legs to base of body, using thread double. Seam of leg faces back of body and pile of fur fabric strokes from hip to foot. Start and finish on outside of each leg and sew round twice.

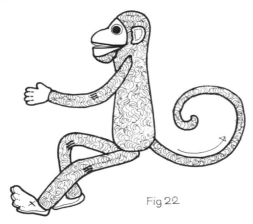

Fig 22

Fig. 22 Bend each arm at elbow and each leg at knee. A crease forms. Using thread double, ladder stitch along this crease as shown by dotted line from one side of arm along front of arm to other side and from one side of knee along back of knee to other side. This holds arms and legs in bent position. Arms and legs can be left straight if preferred.

Hands Using brown thread double, ladder stitch a hand to end of

105

each arm. Thumb points upwards. Ladder stitch twice round wrist.

Feet Using brown thread double, ladder stitch a foot to end of each leg. Sew twice round leg. If the foot seems to hang down lift up the foot to a good right angle position and sew another row of ladder stitch from side to side across front of foot and leg, sewing higher up on leg. X on fig. 22 shows position.

Tail Using thread double, ladder stitch one end of tail to foot of body, working on back seam. Pile of fur fabric strokes from body to tip of tail. Keep sewing round till tail feels really secure. The wire lets the end of the tail turn up.

Funny Fred

Ask a visitor to shake hands with Funny Fred and give him a surprise. As Fred's hand is shaken his arm grows longer while you open Fred's mouth and make him howl with pain. Have some comedy as Funny Fred realises that his other arm is now too short and blames the visitor. Helpfully you pull the short arm but it now becomes too long while the original arm is too short!

Funny Fred's arms are slotted through holes in the body so that they can be pulled in and out. Most people's handshakes are fairly gentle so, as the visitor takes Fred's hand, be ready to jerk Fred backwards to make sure that the arm does extend.

Funny Fred is an example of a design-it-yourself puppet. He owns Chippy the Chimp's body and wide stiffened mouth, but instead of the built-up padded head and long limbs he is finished off with bulging eyes and short limbs with unusual hands and feet. He is 22 in (55·9 cm) high.

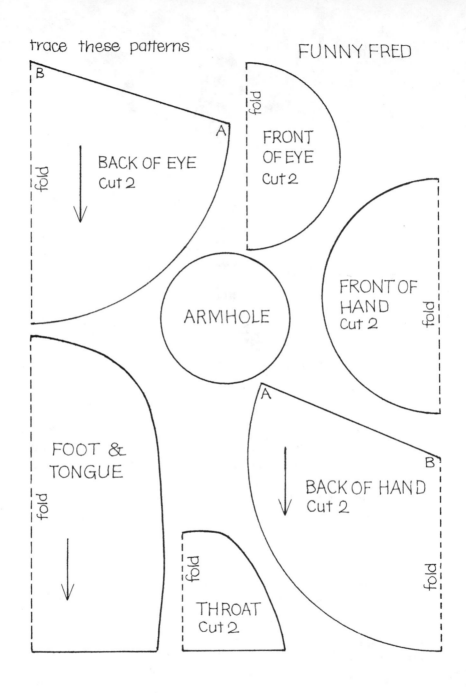

trace these patterns   FUNNY FRED

B

A

BACK OF EYE
Cut 2

fold

FRONT
OF EYE
Cut 2

fold

ARMHOLE

FRONT OF
HAND
Cut 2

fold

FOOT &
TONGUE

fold

A

B

BACK OF HAND
Cut 2

fold

THROAT
Cut 2

fold

MATERIALS

½ yd (50 cm) brown fur fabric, ⅓ yd (30 cm) turquoise blue fabric for mouth, feet and hands, 6 in (20 cm) thin fabric any colour for pads, all at 36 in (90 cm) wide; 9 in × 6 in (22·8 cm × 15·3 cm) cream fabric for inner mouth; small pieces red and black fabric; two pieces each 4 in (10·2 cm) square stiff card or plastic from detergent container for stiffening mouth; two joggle eyes; stuffing and thread in brown, red and black.

PATTERNS

Trace the patterns given. Also use the patterns from Chippy the Chimp for body, p. 83, inner mouth, upper mouth, lower mouth and mouth stiffener card, page 93, finger pocket and thumb pocket, page 95, making patterns from squared diagrams as described at front of book.

Brown fur fabric Cut out two bodies but do not cut out the armhole, one circle 5½ in (14 cm) in diameter, two backs of eyes, two backs of hands, two feet, one piece 17 in × 3 in (43·2 cm × 7·6 cm) for arm and two pieces each 7 in × 3 in (17·8 cm × 7·6 cm) for legs. On arms and legs pile of fur fabric strokes along the length. *Turquoise blue fabric* One upper mouth, one lower mouth, two fronts of eyes, two fronts of hands, two feet, one finger pocket, one thumb pocket and four mouth stiffener covers which are obtained by cutting paper pattern for 'mouth stiffener card' and cutting the fabric ¼ in (6 mm) larger all round. *Cream fabric* One inner mouth. *Red fabric* One tongue. *Black fabric* Two throats. *Pad fabric* Two circles each 5½ in (14 cm) in diameter and one piece 18 in × 6 in (45·7 cm × 15·3 cm). *Card or plastic* Two mouth stiffeners as pattern. *Paper* One armhole from body pattern.

SEWING

All backstitch is done ¼ in (6 mm) from edge.

Throat Fig. 1 Fold each black throat piece in half, wrong side to outside. Backstitch along curved side. Round opening turn edge to wrong side and tack down. Turn to right side.

Tongue Fig. 2 Turn edges of red tongue to wrong side and tack down. Lay cream inner mouth right side uppermost. Crease it to find the centre line, shown dotted. Pin tongue just below centre line and two black throat pieces just above centre line. Folded sides of throat pieces face each other. Sew round edge of each piece with small hemming stitches in red or black.

Copy Chippy the Chimp Funny Fred's mouth is the same as the Chimp's mouth. Follow instructions from Chimp p. 97 paragraph beginning MOUTH. Make sure that upper mouth links with the throat pieces on inner mouth while lower mouth links with the tongue. Carry on till p. 99 end of paragraph titled CHECKING.

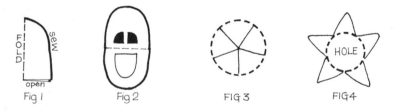

Fig I   Fig 2   FIG 3   FIG 4

BODY

Armhole Fig. 3 Body pattern shows position for armhole. Mark it on wrong side of fur fabric body and lay paper pattern of armhole at this place. Backstitch just outside edge of paper circle. Remove paper. From centre of circle cut five lines radiating to the sewing.

Fig. 4 Fold back each segment to wrong side. Sew down round edge of each segment. Try not to take stitches through to right side. This leaves a circular hole in the body through which the arm can be pulled.

Copy Chippy the Chimp Funny Fred's body is the same as the

Chimp's body. Follow instructions from p. 99 paragraph beginning BODY. Carry on to p. 100, end of paragraph titled MOUTH INTO BODY.

BODY PAD

Fold the long strip of pad fabric in half and sew the short sides together to form a circle. Pin, then sew, a pad fabric circle into each end. Leave an opening in one circle. When stuffing keep circles as flat as possible. Slip pad into foot of body. Working on inside of body use brown thread to sew the top to the front and back seams of body.

EYES AND HANDS

Fig. 5 Fold each fur fabric back of eye and back of hand in half, wrong side to outside. Using thread double backstitch AB. Use the thread double and sew a joggle eye to the centre of each blue front of eye. Pin a front of eye into open end of fur eye and a blue front of hand into open end of fur hand. Using brown thread double, backstitch in place, leaving an opening of about 2 in (5·1 cm) for stuffing. Round opening turn edges to wrong side and tack down. Turn to right side. Stuff and ladder stitch to close hole.

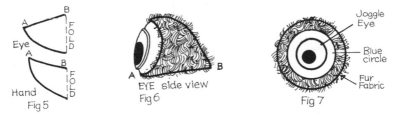

Figs. 6 and 7 show finished eye. Finished hand looks similar but without the eye on the blue circle.

ARMS, LEGS AND FEET

Fold the arm and each leg piece in half lengthwise. Tack them. Using thread double backstitch the long side leaving an opening for stuffing. Round opening turn edges $\frac{1}{4}$ in (6 mm) to wrong side and tack down. Using thread double gather each short end. Pull up and finish off thread. Turn to right side. Stuff, working from each end to finish at middle. Ladder stitch to close opening.

Pin one blue foot and one brown fur fabric foot together, wrong sides to outside. Using brown thread double, backstitch together, leaving curved end open for stuffing. Round opening turn edges $\frac{1}{4}$ in (6 mm) to wrong side and tack down. Turn to right side. Stuff and ladder stitch to close opening.

Mark toes Use black thread double and take stitches about $\frac{1}{2}$ in (1·2 cm) long going right through foot and back on under side. Pull each stitch tight and go over it three times to make a thick black line. Sew three lines to make four toes as shown on fig. 9.

ASSEMBLY

Eyes to head Fig 8 Sew eyes to head using brown thread double. Eyes face straight ahead, about $\frac{1}{2}$ in (1·2 cm) above the mouth and stick up in the air. Seam AB of eye lies on head. Ladder stitch eye to body along front of eye where it touches body then along each side of AB. Sew round a second time.

Fig 8

Hands to arm Fig. 8 Using thread double sew a hand to one end of the arm. Place point B of hand to end of arm. Ladder stitch round

112

at least three times till hand sits firmly on arm. Push the other end of the arm into one armhole of the body and out through the other armhole. Sew the second hand to this end of arm. The arm can be pulled backwards and forwards through the holes but the wide hands make sure that arm cannot be pulled out of body.

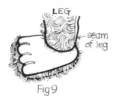

Fig 9

Feet to legs Fig. 9 Blue fabric is upper side of foot, with fur underneath. Place end of leg on top of foot with seam of leg to back. Pile of fur on leg strokes from top of leg to foot. Using brown thread double, ladder stitch twice round leg.

Legs to body Hold body and leg upside down. Using thread double, ladder stitch top of leg to base of body. Feet point to front. Sew round twice.

Dressing the Puppets

There are three methods of dressing puppets.

1. MAKING SEPARATE CLOTHES

Remember that clothes must be designed to give the puppeteer's hand access to the opening in the body.

2. CLOTHES AS PART OF PUPPET

The puppet's body, arms and legs are made in dress fabric with head, hands and feet in fur fabric. Thus the puppet looks dressed but the clothes cannot come off. Make extra paper patterns and cut them where required. Allow $\frac{1}{4}$ in (6 mm) turning at each cut. Backstitch the cut pieces together and then follow the original instructions for that puppet. This is an excellent way of using small pieces of fabric left over from the other puppets.

Fig 1   Fig 2   Fig 3

Figs. 1 and 2 show ways of using fabrics to get shirt and trouser effects. On fig. 3 the body is made in dress fabric from shoulder to hips and a skirt is added when puppet is finished. Legs are cut to

114

give short socks and bare knees, with 'shoes' instead of feet. Sleeves can be short or long according to where the cut is made.

3. ODD BITS OF CLOTHING

On an undressed puppet create the impression of being dressed by adding an item such as a scarf, collar and tie or fancily-shaped collar. Drape headsquares, handkerchiefs, belts, fringing and oddments of fabric in various ways, either tacking them temporarily or holding with safety pins hidden from view.

Design Your Own Puppets

BIRDS

All birds have roughly the same shape with a protruding beak. So make practically any bird you wish by choosing the nearest pattern and making it in suitable colours. Notice in the book how one body turns into Crow, Owl or Penguin.

WHICH BIRD AM I?

MISS CHIMP

ANIMALS

Choose the animal pattern that has the nearest shape of head to the one you wish to design. Make it in suitable colour and fabric and add new ears and tail. With the added dimension of the voice, such as a cow that moos, most audiences will accept it!

Make a wig from wool. Sew the wool to a fabric foundation that can be tacked to the puppet's head to make a humanized animal.

116

IMAGINATIVE CREATURES

These really give you scope. Take any body pattern and add eyes,
ears, tail and limbs of your own design or taken from other puppets.
Dozens of weird creatures can result, as shown by Funny Fred who
is the foundation of the chimp with new bits added.

List of Mail Order Craft Suppliers

FRED ALDOUS LTD The Handcraft Centre, PO Box 135, 37 Lever Street, Manchester M60 1UX
  Fur fabric, stuffing, joggle eyes.

A. BYWATER LTD Portland Mills, Reinwood Road, Lindley, Huddersfield
  Fur fabric.

DRYAD Northgates, Leicester LE1 4QR
  Fur fabric, stuffing.

NEEDLECRAFT AND HOBBIES 83 Northgate, Canterbury, Kent
  Stuffing, joggle eyes.

FLUFFY FABRICS 26/28 Tribune Drive, Trinity Trading Estate, Sittingbourne, Kent
  Fur fabric.

HOME HANDICRAFTS 9 Uplands Close, Cannock Wood, Rugeley, Staffs.
  Fur fabric.

OAKLEY FABRICS LTD 62/64 Collingdon Street, Luton, Beds.
  Fur fabric.